RUNNING
THROUGH FIRE

THE NEA HERITAGE & PRESERVATION SERIES

CELEBRATES THE MULTICULTURAL DIVERSITY OF AMERICAN
LETTERS WITH MODERN CLASSICS OF CULTURAL IDENTITY.

ALSO IN THIS SERIES:

JOSÉ ANTONIO BURCIAGA
IN FEW WORDS/EN POCAS PALABRAS
A Compendium of Latino Folk Wit & Wisdom

CHARLES WRIGHT
THE WIG

SADAKICHI HARTMANN
A SADAKICHI HARTMANN READER

RUNNING THROUGH FIRE

HOW I SURVIVED THE HOLOCAUST

BY ZOSIA GOLDBERG

AS TOLD TO HILTON OBENZINGER

WITH AN INTRODUCTION BY PAUL AUSTER

 MERCURY HOUSE   SAN FRANCISCO

Published in the United States by Mercury House, San Francisco, California, a
nonprofit publishing company devoted to the free exchange of ideas and guided by
a dedication to literary values. Mercury House and colophon are registered trade-
marks of Mercury House, Incorporated. Visit us at: mercuryhouse.org

United States Constitution, First Amendment: Congress shall make no law re-
specting an establishment of religion, or prohibiting the free exercise thereof;
or abridging the freedom of speech, or of the press; or the right of the people
peaceably to assemble, and to petition the Government for a redress of grievances.

Cover design—Scott di Girolamo
Cover art—*top:* Zosia Goldberg, date unknown;
bottom: "SS Troops walk past a block of burning housing during the suppression of
the Warsaw Ghetto uprising, April 19–May 16, 1943"; U.S. Holocaust Memorial
Museum, courtesy of National Archives.
Map (page 174)—published by permission of Martin Gilbert, author of *Atlas of the
Holocaust,* Third edition (Routledge, London and New York, 2002).

*The NEA Heritage & Preservation Series celebrates the multicultural diversity of American
letters with modern classics of cultural identity. We thank the National Endowment for the
Arts for their continued support. We also wish to thank Jeremy Lindston, Mark M.
Obenzinger, and Zosia's son Steven and his wife Tracy for additional support.*

Copyedited by Jeanne Storck. Printed on acid-free paper and manufactured in the
United States of America by Sheridan Books, Ann Arbor, Michigan.

Library of Congress Cataloging in Publication Data:

Goldberg, Zosia.
    Running through fire : how I survived the Holocaust /
by Zosia Goldberg as told to Hilton Obenzinger ;
with an introduction by Paul Auster.– 1st American Paperback ed.
        p. cm. – (NEA heritage & preservation series ; 3)
    ISBN 1-56279-128-1 (pbk. : alk. paper)
  1. Goldberg, Zosia. 2. Jews–Poland–Warsaw–Biography.
3. Holocaust, Jewish (1939–1945)–Poland–Warsaw–Personal narratives.
4. Warsaw (Poland)–Biography. I. Obenzinger, Hilton. II. Title. III. Series.
    DS135.P63.G6394   2004
    940.53'18'092–dc22

                                        2004000558

TO MY PARENTS—

ESPECIALLY MY FATHER

Stefania and Mieczyslaw Goldberg in Lublin—1938

CONTENTS

Zosia Goldberg—Warsaw, 1938

PREFACE

BY HILTON OBENZINGER

I had always heard Zosia's stories growing up, or half heard. Often she would remember an incident but not tell it all, or she would blurt it out to my parents in Polish I could not understand, or she would only refer to nightmares. But, in fragments, I began to learn of the particular ordeal she had to endure to survive the Nazi onslaught against Europe and the Jews.

Years later I decided to record my aunt's story from beginning to end so I could finally determine some sense of the real dimensions of Hitler's murder of my family, to extract them from the nightmares I had growing up of ovens and bones, the photographs of people standing like skeletons behind barbed wire. This mania to know, to comprehend the totality of such horror, became part of writing an earlier book. In the spring of 1979, we recorded seventeen hours of tape as Zosia and I walked up and down the tree-lined streets of Valley Stream, Long Island, a suburb right outside New York City, or sat alongside her dining-room table over the course of many days. We walked and she talked. I prodded some, but once she began to talk the problem was rarely faulty memory, but a rush of details, the confluence of so many sub-plots with the immensity of the brutality, ugliness, pain. Her telling, and the childhood legend of it in my own psyche, contributed to my earlier book, yet the need to know remained, and grew.

Sofia (Zosia) Goldberg, my mother's sister, came from an assimilated Jewish family in Warsaw. Her father had fought with Pilsudski for Polish independence, and he was the highest Jewish civil servant in the Polish government. Zosia never knew Yiddish, and she had even gone to Gentile schools and learned Catholic prayers. As the roundups and deportations mounted in the Warsaw Ghetto, she tried to think of ways to save herself and her mother. Hearing noises, she ran down the stairs of her apartment to find out if the Germans were on their way to clear out their building. An old, bearded man, startled at hearing her speak in Polish, screamed something at her in Yiddish. Zosia ran upstairs to her mother to find out what the man had said, and her mother exclaimed, "Who told you this curse?" The old man had said, *"May you die amongst the goyim!"* It was his utterance of disgust at what to him was my aunt's starkly un-Jewish manner, but Zosia took it not as a curse but as the voice of God. *She would survive by escaping to the Aryan side of the walls to pose as a non-Jew.* Eventually, she purposely allowed herself to be captured as a Pole to be taken to Germany for forced labor. She calculated that life on the streets of Warsaw would be too dangerous; the safest place for her to hide would be as a Gentile in the heart of Germany itself.

And so, Zosia's story of survival takes place in the ghetto, the streets of "Aryan" Warsaw, and several sites for forced labor in Germany. She eluded going to any of the death camps, yet she did witness the brunt of the Nazi destruction of the Warsaw Ghetto. And, as a Jew hiding amongst Polish, Ukrainian, and Russian workers, French POWs, and the many others forced into labor by the Third Reich, Zosia was also able to see some of the violence done to the other peoples of Europe. She also lived amongst the German civilians, the small farmers, the bureaucrats and technicians. And she came to know the Gestapo and other Nazi interrogators and torturers the several times she was captured after attempted escapes.

She avoided certain death many times because she was a young, shrewd, and beautiful woman. She was also courageous. She learned early on that, in order to hide her true identity, she could show no fear, that fear in the face of an interrogator or even torture was as good as a confession: "Once you were in their hands, and once you showed them you were scared, you were finished." She would curse, accuse her accusers, and even confess to lesser crimes in order to cover up the far more serious "crime" of being Jewish.

But mainly she avoided death because of luck. She would run through the gunfire of "actions" and roundups for the cattle trains inexplicably unscathed. Using the French term to describe herself, she was a *débrouillarde,* someone who was resourceful, who could run through fire without getting burned. It is such luck that most perplexes a survivor like Zosia. So very often she could have died, and should have, given all logic—and so many did die, no matter how smart, courageous, or beautiful. The morning after American tanks liberated that part of Germany where she had worked, she stretched outdoors to exult in her new freedom, and a hidden Nazi suddenly cocked his rifle—even then, having survived the entire war, she should have died. The fact that she did not die there—or in the ghetto or on the streets of Warsaw or when she was tortured by the Gestapo—remains the kind of thing that renders the nature of life and of evil more mysterious and impossible to comprehend.

Years after these tapes were recorded I decided to produce this book, if for no other reason than to give it to the next generation of our family, to Zosia's son, my own son, and my brother's children. Virtually all that remains of both of my parent's extensive families, they are the ones who need to know and to preserve her story. I had the hours of tape transcribed, I edited and adapted them, rearranged the narrative in chronological order, and did everything to make the story known. Still, in great part I produced this document because of that mania that is a legacy of the Nazi murders handed to the children or, in my case, to the close relatives of survivors—that mania to make it knowable, to have those vague whispers in Polish during my own childhood become hard, spoken English, a compulsion that probably would not be felt by others, at least not in the same way.

I prodded, but she spoke. And, while I have corrected grammar and rearranged sentences, I have kept Zosia's basic idiom, an English buffeted by Polish, German, French, even by the Spanish she learned when, after first living in the United States for some fifteen years, she moved with her late husband to Caracas, Venezuela, in the early sixties.

Zosia spoke, prodding me. She was particularly anxious that her story might be misunderstood. "I talk so much about Germans who saved me and Jews who were collaborators and denouncers. I don't say enough who did the killing, how much the Nazis were killing," she would tell me the several times we edited this book together. I believe her story quite clearly shows how monstrous were the Nazis; but it also shows how some Jews coped with the impossible situation with utmost selfishness, and how there were some German soldiers and officials who were capable of helping. Still, Zosia remains concerned that too many exceptions may have unmade the rule. I don't think this is the case, her anxiety over the point only underscoring the horror even more starkly.

Yet another problematic situation we have had to contend with has been the response of the publishing world. Although the book was originally intended for private use, friends urged me to send it to publishers, arguing that the narrative deserved a broader public. But as we sent drafts of this book to different publishers, we received surprising replies that were far stranger than the usual "this book is very moving, but it does not fit our publishing focus" or "the market's flooded with this stuff right now." As dismaying as such responses to an account of actual horror may be, there were others far more disturbing.

One publisher thought the story was very compelling, but felt that the book required "more character development." It seemed to make no difference when I reminded this editor that the book was not fiction but oral history. Zosia's narrative reads like fiction, so therefore it demanded better treatment as fiction, in this editor's eyes. Despite the constant anxiety by survivors that their stories would not be believed, this editor *wanted* it to become fiction. While his confusion seemed to testify to the narrative power of Zosia's voice, expanded "character development" is not an element of her account.

Another publisher responded that the book was "incredible; in fact, too incredible. After forty or so years, she may be exaggerating. I don't mean that she's lying, but … Well, even if she *is* lying, it still could be an interesting book. In fact, it might be even more interesting …" This editor recommended that I have the manuscript reviewed by academics to verify its authenticity. Such a response—not to be believed—is the survivor's bane, and Zosia was saddened, disheartened. For my part, it little matters whether the names of cities are all correct, or whether all the details of her narrative are chronologically precise, or whether events are slightly distorted by time and personality, although I do believe her story is substantially accurate—her remembrances remain vivid and precise—and it is substantiated by other accounts. What matters more deeply is the story's basic truth, the telling of what a survivor knows, and, as has been argued by others, "testimony" as a form of oral literature is validity enough. But it so happens, in the course of pursuing publication in the U.K., the manuscript was shown to Rafael Scharf in London. Scharf, a Holocaust scholar and Polish Jewish survivor himself, validated the authenticity of Zosia's account.

As these examples show, the search for a publisher became part of the legacy of Zosia's story. Eventually, I gave up, printing the document for our family's use only, letting the matter rest for a decade. However, Paul Auster had been impressed by Zosia's story when he read it years ago, and when I visited him in the fall of 2000, he suggested that I try again, and he agreed to write an introduction to help secure publication. This time we succeeded.

Zosia and I have our differences—age, cultural background, political views—yet she told her story to me, willingly confided in me, returning to the hideous fear that had never entirely left her after so many years. I listened, we worked together crafting this document, and a bond was formed no matter what *we* think: The memory is important in and of itself. We feel a need to make sure that people know, a need that eclipses what we may think about the story itself or the dilemmas of today. What the world does with the story is an entirely different matter, a serious one, but one that is beyond our powers. Glad that at least we could make this document, we can only hope for life.

This book came about because of the help of many people who should be mentioned here. Most especially, Paul Auster for his dedication to storytelling of all kinds, and for his persistence in bringing Zosia's story to the public. Stephen Vincent for transcribing the tapes with a poet's ear, and for his considerable creative input and insistence on making the book a reality. Kirsten Janene-Nelson and everyone associated with Mercury House for the courage and vision to publish Zosia's story. Steven, Zosia's son, for gathering photographs and facilitating the book's production. Mark Obenzinger, my brother, who grew up also hearing these stories and who assisted with the means to complete the book. My parents Nathan and Romana Obenzinger for their support, particularly as many of the interviews were done in the streets by their home. My wife, Estella Habal, for understanding my nightmares and mania. And, of course, Zosia, for her wit, determination, and patience.

Hilton Obenzinger
San Francisco–Stanford, California
1990–2004

INTRODUCTION

BY PAUL AUSTER

I thought fast. I was lucky and got an idea. These two short sentences come toward the end of Zosia Goldberg's remarkable account of how she managed to live through the nightmare years of the Second World War, and they encapsulate the spirit of the entire story she tells us. Like a female Odysseus, this beautiful and resourceful young woman needed more than simple courage to overcome the dangers that surrounded her. Survival demanded cunning, quick thinking under pressure, a ferocious will to adapt to the most frightening and intolerable conditions, and sheer dumb luck—a chance encounter with the right person at the right moment, removal from one prison to another just hours before the first prison was bombed, an endless series of small, unfathomable miracles.

Why did some live when so many millions died? In Zosia Goldberg's case, it seems to have been the result of a rare and fortuitous constellation of circumstances. She was a woman, which gave her the possibility of posing as a Gentile—an option not available to Jewish men—and she came from a highly assimilated secular family. Polish was the language spoken at home, not Yiddish, and therefore she could speak without having to worry that her accent would give her away. But beyond these accidents of birth and language, there was the question of character. Although just twenty-one when the Germans invaded Poland, Zosia Goldberg was no longer a girl, and to hear her talk about her experiences to her nephew, Hilton Obenzinger, she was no ordinary person. Stubborn, opinionated, sexy, fearless, with a clairvoyant's ability to read and judge the intentions of other people, she had an unbending trust in her own instincts. Early in her story, for example, when an ex-boyfriend proposes to escape from the ghetto with her and find shelter in the Aryan section of Warsaw, she hesitates. "Should I or shouldn't I?" she tells her nephew. "First of all, he was not faithful to me. He was never faithful. If he was not faithful in love, he would not be faithful for more important matters like life and death. This type of fellow I did not need."

On the other hand, she never deluded herself into thinking she could survive without the help of others. One of the most disturbing aspects of this book is where Zosia Goldberg sometimes found that help. At several perilous junctures she was aided by older German soldiers (the young ones were invariably die-hard Nazis, she discovered), and in some of those instances, even after her Jewish identity had been exposed, these men did not betray her. This contradicts nearly everything we have been told about German conduct during the war, and when you factor in the additional help she received from working-class Poles, and then combine that with the various examples she mentions of Jews betraying other Jews, the stark black-and-white picture we have drawn of the Holocaust dissolves into a muddled, terrifying gray—a world in which humanity carried on with its usual greeds and lusts, its occasional flashes of goodness and self-sacrifice, its eternal unpredictability. In one chilling passage about conditions in the ghetto, Zosia Goldberg tells us: "People hated each other. You understand, they were starving. They could kill each other for food. We had a family from Lodz in our apartment. My mother cooked. The wife of this man came and ate up my mother's soup, so my mother complained to me. The man did not like my mother complaining, so he pushed her around and beat her up. When I came home from work that day I hit him on the head with an iron pot. I got even for my mother. He got no pity from me. He never touched her anymore." And then, one paragraph down on the same page: "We were so demoralized that people became disrespectful of each other. If a married man had a sweetheart, he brought her to his house, and the wife was lucky if he did not throw her out on the street. If he gave his wife food and a place to sleep on the floor, she was considered lucky."

Eventually, Zosia Goldberg slipped out of the ghetto by way of the sewers, got herself captured on purpose, and was shipped to Germany, where she spent the rest of the war doing forced labor—in a munitions factory and on a number of farms. Every day carried the threat of denunciation, of arrest and torture, of death. But she had been given some good advice by one of her father's Gentile friends before leaving the ghetto, and she learned her lessons well. "Remember one thing," the man told her. "When somebody attacks you, never show fear. Use vulgar words like anybody else, the most dirty words so that you sound sure of yourself. And attack *them!*" The point being, as she explains to her nephew, "... if a German beats you up and you don't fight back, that means you are a Jew, that you are scared. A Gentile always strikes back."

Knowing that things could turn against her at any moment, she was constantly prepared for the worst. "I had long hair tied in a knot at the back. I had razor blades hidden in the knot in order to commit suicide in case I could not take it anymore." But Zosia Goldberg never succumbed to despair. She was interrogated by the Gestapo and badly beaten; she was often close to starvation; she suffered from hepatitis, from mange itch, from lice; and at one point she felt that her spirit had finally been broken. But it wasn't. In the end, I believe that was her most transcendent accomplishment—as great, if not greater, than the fact that she survived. *Running Through Fire* is a book filled with unspeakable horrors—but it is told without a shred of self-pity. Zosia Goldberg never complains, never bemoans her lot. She battles and endures, and in this raw, unvarnished tale of human suffering, she has given us a manual of hope.

Paul Auster
Brooklyn, New York
July 2003

RUNNING THROUGH FIRE

Mieczyslaw Goldberg, highest Jewish official in the Polish
government, at his desk—Warsaw, c. 1935

BEFORE THE WAR

My father, Mieczyslaw Goldberg, was once the director of a very big factory. He was director probably because it was a Jewish-owned firm. Everything was fine until World War I when the business suddenly moved to Russia and he was left without a job. It was the worst of times in Poland. No jobs, no money, people were hungry. It was a depression.

The political atmosphere in Poland was bad. Parties like *Endecja* and *Obwiepole* were strictly anti-Semitic and nationalistic, against the Jews and all minorities. They were making trouble for Marshall Josef Pilsudski, the leader of Poland at the time. Pilsudski was a fine democratic man, although some people believe he was a dictator. But I think Marshall Pilsudski was the greatest man Poland had in this time. He created a united and independent Poland after World War I.

I grew up in Warsaw, where I first went to a Catholic elementary school. Roma, my sister, and I were the only two Jewish students. We were very assimilated. I knew that I was Jewish, but it was not such a big deal. When I went to this school I even studied Catholic religion, and I learned without trying too hard. Whenever the priest gave lessons to the children, I was there, too. Not that I really wanted to study or be Catholic, but during the hour for religion there was nothing else for me to do.

School was fine until one day the other children were going to church, to communion, and I wanted to go, too. But one of the girls said, "Where are you going, you Jew! You don't go anywhere!"

The teacher of my class called my father and said, "Look, you have to know one thing. Your children are Jewish and they are suffering in a non-Jewish school. There are no Jewish children except them and they are mistreated, which I don't like. I believe they should go to a school where there are Jewish children." She was really a wonderful person. I even remember her name, Cieslinska. I loved her very much.

So father took us out and put us in a private school, a *gymnasium* that was owned by Jews where the teachers and the students were all Jews. But since I was accustomed to eating ham with matzos and learning from the kids how to say "Jesus, Maria" and so on, the Jewish children were soon calling me a *goy*.

That was no good either. So my father turned to another school where the children were all Jewish and the teachers were mixed, some Gentiles and some Jews, and this school was much better. Studies were very strict, but there were no problems for us anymore.

We were poor. In those times everyone was poor, but we were extremely poor because my father had no job. Then in about 1929 my father, Uncle Philip Lebenbaum, and a cousin of my mother, Lutek Trauman, all started to work for the government. Lutek was a big philosopher, always philosophizing about the home, life, and the world. They all worked in the Ministry of Justice or the Ministry of the Interior, I do not know exactly. Then Philip went to America and Lutek stopped working, but my father stayed on. He worked his way up to a position in the Ministry of the Exterior, dealing with passports and things like that.

He could easily enter anyone's files. As a matter of fact, he helped plenty of Jews. He helped our cousin Hela Strumfeld, who was a communist. She ran into some trouble, and she could have gone to a concentration camp. There was one camp before the war, called *Bereza Kartuska,* and all the people who were busy with politics, especially the communists, wound up there. Once they were there they could not get out so easily. My father simply took all the papers from her files, and then she did not exist anymore and no police, nobody, could ever check on her—although afterward she was caught on the street once with quite incriminating papers.

Before the First World War, my father was in the underground and fought for the independence of Poland. As a matter of fact, he knew Marshall Pilsudski personally. He knew all the big people. If somebody wanted to go to school to be a doctor and could not because of the *numerus clausus*—the restrictive quotas that excluded Jews—my father, with his many acquaintances, could manage to get him into medical school.

He was the highest Jewish civil servant. There were two or three Jews who were congressmen in the *Sejm,* the Polish parliament. They would give speeches, saying the Jews were not being treated right, but the other congressmen made such a noise, knocking gavels on their desks, that nobody heard them. Those Jews were there, in the *Sejm,* but they could do nothing.

My father was a loyal citizen, a patriot, and he proved himself in the fight for the independence of Poland. Other Jews stayed on the sideline, not doing much. The anti-Semitism was tremendous. My father's looks happened to be so Gentile that the Gentiles were always asking, "Are you Jewish? Are you sure?" They would not believe him, always saying he was not Jewish, and he would get very angry. Toward the thirties, the situation for him had gotten so bad that they demoted him. He was going down, down, down. He had his friends, but he was not important anymore. They mistreated him, and he suffered very much. Naturally, it was because the influence of Hitler was radiating and penetrating Poland.

People in his family were all blond, all blue-eyed, and spoke Polish, not Yiddish. He was Bar Mitzvahed, and they celebrated all the Jewish holidays, but they did not go to the synagogue, except on Yom Kippur. They were quite assimilated. They spoke French, German, Russian, but they never spoke Yiddish. You see, they considered themselves Poles, they did not consider themselves Jews. They knew they were Jews. They were not against the Jews or anything like that, but they were assimilated Jews. In the U.S. you would call them Reform Jews.

When they came around to take the census, you had to write nationality, religion, and so forth. When they asked "What nationality are you?" many Jews wrote "Jew." What religion? They wrote, "Jewish." But my father wrote his nationality was Polish and his religion, Jewish. He felt he was a Pole. But he also had dreams of going to Palestine, to make an army, to organize the country. He dreamt about it whenever he felt anti-Semitism on his job.

Besides that, he sympathized with the workers' party; he was a socialist. He sympathized with the Jewish Workers *Bund,* even though it was Yiddish-oriented. In the beginning he was a member of the Polish Socialist Party, but later as a government employee he was not allowed to be in any party. My father always voted for the government party, Pilsudski's party, because he was a democrat and a socialist.

Our family on both sides had been in Poland for centuries. They were there from the time Jews were allowed into Poland in the Middle Ages by King Kazimierz Wielki, Casimir the Great, who invited them in. The king wanted to develop commerce, and the Polish people did not know how to work the trades. They did not even know how to make a shoe.

My mother's mother died very young, at age thirty-nine, from diabetes. All her family on her mother's side were Jews who were not as assimilated as my father's family, but they were still quite assimilated. They were not very religious, and all of them were rather well-to-do. Some were doctors, quite educated, and they were doing all right in

Poland. Her uncle was extremely wealthy, a millionaire, although on her side of the family there were very poor people, too. Quite a mixture. Only my mother's father was religious. He was a very religious Jew with a big beard. I remember him as a lovely person.

When I was going to school, I had feelings for communism, like all the young ones. My father said, "Now look, until you are of age, don't get into any party. You are not supposed to, and you will get us into trouble. I don't want it, and I won't permit it." No party whatsoever, he did not even permit me to join the Zionist party, although my sister was then secretly going to meetings of *Hashomer Hatzair,* the Zionist labor party. I was learning Hebrew songs from her. The Zionists would march in Warsaw, preparing themselves to go to Palestine. Many of them did go and managed to survive the war.

My feelings were strong over Spain, Franco, the Spanish Civil War. I would stand with a Spanish flag in front of the school. "Death to Franco! Long live the Republic!" I was almost thrown out of school, but my father said to them, "Look, she's a child, she does not know what she's doing. How can you throw her out? If you do, she could never enter any other school." This was true especially since the government was paying for my school, not my father. They did not throw me out.

The situation in Poland got worse when Pilsudski died in 1935, a few years before the war started. We knew that Pilsudski was in love with a Jewish woman when he was fighting for the independence of Poland. This Jewish woman saved his life, and he really loved her, more than the wife he married later on. He was always on the side of the Jews. All the other nationalist parties—I would call them Nazi parties—they were always saying, "Pilsudski, the grandfather of the Jews." They hated him for that. Only the workers remained loyal to Pilsudski.

My sister Roma left Poland in 1935. Just before she left, she had started working in the Army, in the medication unit. She had gotten the job through my father. A good friend of my father was a major who used to live in our house in the country. He said, "Don't worry, I will give her a job." She got the job, but it required she go to Prague and pretend she was a Gentile. She did not like that, so she refused and said, "I don't want to stay in this anti-Semitic Poland. I have to get out." She wanted to go to Palestine, but our Aunt Mania Lebenbaum, my mother's sister in America, wrote a letter saying to send Roma there for a visit. She would get her to America so she would never have to come back. So my father went to the American embassy and gave his word of honor that she would come back because she had a boyfriend and other things that were not true. He lied to get her out as fast as possible, and she got to America this way.

In 1937, I graduated from the *gymnasium,* the same as graduating from two years of college. After graduating I married Marian Merenholtz, a musician who was also sympathetic to communism, although he was not an activist. My parents approved the marriage, although my mother did not like his profession. But it didn't last, and we divorced after less than a year.

All the American songs were very popular then. We were singing songs like "America, USA, It's a Country of Paradise." There was a popular dance called the Lambeth Walk. Everybody at the time was thinking *America, America, America*—they thought their one hope was America.

We went out to the nightclubs and cafés. Life was just tremendous in Warsaw. Everybody lived like it was the last days of Pompeii. It's a funny thing, but when my sister, Roma, and her husband, Nathan, came back to visit us in 1938, they told us we better go to America; they said, "Run, run, run, the Germans are marching," but we were not even thinking of leaving. The Jews in Poland did not believe something would happen to them. They dared not think something would happen, although the signs were very clear. There were two writers who wrote, in a newspaper called *Nasz Pszegland,* a daily column with the title "Poland Without the Jews." I think their names were Apenszlak and Szwalbe. They predicted everything that would happen in Poland, what life in Poland would be like without the Jews. I don't know how they imagined the lack of Jews in Poland, but that's just what ended up happening.

I did not suffer much, but the Jews in Poland did. Especially if you had a Jewish accent and could not speak Polish, people would always say hurtful things, like: "Dirty Jew." With my dark eyes and hair, I never heard that I was a Jew. They called me a Gypsy instead—admiringly!

I did not suffer, but that does not mean I did not see other Jews suffering. My cousin, Zygmunt Warszawski, was such a good student he got into the University of Warsaw to study engineering, which for a Jew was a big achievement because of the *numerus clausus* that limited the number of Jews allowed in. The Gentile students at the university would beat up Jews, forcing them to stand all day on one side, and if they tried to sit somewhere else, they would get beaten up again. The police would be outside, but because of the pretext that the police could not enter the university, they could not help the Jews. My cousin was beaten up so badly I was surprised he did not have some kind of internal injury. He became quite sick. Even though he was from the same assimilated family, that did not help.

I was twenty-one when the war started in September 1939. The invasion of Poland began on the first of September, and the bombing of Warsaw started soon after that. And the third of September was my birthday! But before that—a week or two weeks before—President Moscicki spoke on the radio to the people, crying, and said: "I am very sorry, but we will be attacked soon by the Germans."

Actually, the government had sold out. Beck, who was Minister of the Exterior, was making deals with the Germans. I don't know what kind of deals, but it was not good. Poland was sold out.

Before the German invasion the whole population was so patriotic we did not even realize that all we had was horses to fight against tanks. We were not prepared at all. There was a film just before the war called *J'Accuse,* a French film, I think, which was shown in America, too. In this film they accused the Nazis of all the things that they were doing. And the funniest thing was that before they showed it, they showed newsreels of our cavalry, our infantry marching, and we left the theater, walking and marching on Marszalkowska Street, singing that we wanted to go to Germany to kill the Nazis and so forth. A few days later Germany invaded Poland, but even then we did not realize we were in such danger.

THE SIEGE OF WARSAW

When the Germans bombed Warsaw, we were at our villa in the country, our summer home. My father went back to Warsaw immediately and my mother and I followed him as soon as we could. When we returned, we found soldiers stationed on our roofs. We prepared water and food, tomatoes, sardines, and my mother made marmalade, so we had a lot of sweets, and we had water in the tub. The other neighbors did not have any water or food. They had not prepared themselves.

The government called up the soldiers. My father had fallen ill just before the war with high blood pressure, but he did not want to leave his job because he would lose his pension. He was afraid to be without money. He had struggled all his life, and he did not want to leave his job. But he was so sick that he had been in bed the whole summer. He came back to Warsaw when the war began and went straight to his office in the government.

They decided to take all the treasury—the money—and all the important papers so they would not fall into German hands. What papers they did not take, they burned.

They wanted to take the treasury and papers to England, so they left in trucks and cars and headed toward Romania. But my father, who was much brighter than his Gentile friends, noticed that there was something wrong with the chauffeur of his car. My father suspected he was a traitor heading toward Russia, and he knew that if they went to Russia they would immediately be shot. The chauffeur was a communist who wanted to take the treasury to the Soviet Union. He was going in the wrong direction, so my father said, "Something bad is going to happen to us. I am getting out right here to go back to Warsaw." Three or four friends went with him, but the rest did not listen. They drove a little bit farther, and my father heard explosions and shooting. They were probably caught by the Russians and shot.

It was a tremendous job to get back to Warsaw because German planes were shooting everyone on the road. Everybody was running, and the Germans were shooting the refugees. They could see the planes. They could even see the pilots' faces. And my father, with his bad heart, was lucky to escape and get back to Warsaw.

But when he returned to the city there was no government anymore. There were no high officers left in the army, only soldiers. So he became the right-hand man of the mayor of Warsaw. If I remember correctly, his name was Mayor Starzynski. The mayor gave orders and my father saw that they were carried out. He had to make sure that people were peaceful and did not kill each other and that the hospitals worked. We were already surrounded on all sides. We could not escape. Whoever was in Warsaw was stuck there. It was a complete siege. Warsaw was enclosed.

The siege lasted one month, one month without water, without telephones. Everything was broken and destroyed, burned. Soldiers were everywhere. We had to have blackouts. The Germans were destroying things according to dates. On Friday and Saturday they hit mostly where the Jews lived. And on Sunday they hit the churches and the sections where more Gentiles lived. They knew Warsaw exactly, every street; they had spies everywhere. They bombed the national shrines. At that time, the Polish people and the Jews were very close because they were in trouble together.

My father got an offer from I do not know whom, but from somebody who could swing it, that the three of us, my father and mother and I, could go to some town as Gentiles with papers made by the government in such a way that we would be completely safe. The Germans could not touch him. But he said, "Where the Jews go, I go." And he did not accept it. He was a patriot, but he was quite Jewish in his heart.

He was by that time a very important person. He was very busy, and I hardly ever saw him. I once tried to bring him food during the siege, because there was none. By the time I got to where he was, running through craters and rubble, everything was lost, the soup and everything. It was a mess.

It was a full-fledged war against civilians. You would walk on the street and the shrapnel could cut off your head. You didn't go out anymore. You had to hide in the basements, so my mother stayed at home.

I was in the Red Cross taking care of the wounded. Nobody wanted to be with the Red Cross. The doctors hid, they were scared, so there were no doctors, no nurses. I knew nothing, only first aid, but I took care of the wounded. I remember a child with a smashed face. I had to somehow bandage an open belly with intestines sticking out. Imagine, this was supposed to be an operation and I had to clean it out. What could I do? I poured alcohol and closed the wound with tape. I could do nothing. We shaved the heads of people because we were afraid of typhus, which is carried by lice, but the people hated me for shaving their heads.

We did not want to surrender. So many people were dying, and there was no food, no water, yet people said they did not want to surrender. Neither Jews nor Gentiles, nobody wanted to surrender. Mayor Starzynski did not want to surrender either. He said he would resist to the end, to the last man.

But all of Poland except Warsaw was already taken. Only one other little spot on the Baltic Sea called Westerplatte still held out, a tiny place. They didn't give in. Then there was a big battle, and the Germans killed everyone. When Westerplatte fell, Warsaw was next.

It's odd, but at the very beginning of the war I was very happy. I joyfully did my job. It was like fun, a change, a big change. I took care of these people, soldiers and so on. In the meantime, the Germans were dropping two kinds of bombs: one burning, making fires, and the other destroying, going through the roofs of the buildings. The population always had sand ready because we realized that water spread the fire. There were always some courageous people, children, going up on the roofs and throwing sand, putting out the fires as best they could.

There was such hunger, you have no idea. We ate horses. The horses were killed on the street. They cut them up and we ate them. And there was no water. We drank the dirty water from the tub. We lived on the first or second floor, and the people came down from above to live with us because it was more secure.

One day I was walking with my mother. I was wearing a fur coat on top of many other dresses, in case a bomb fell and we were left without a house or belongings. We slipped and fell into the big wooden washtub in the courtyard. We had to laugh it was so funny.

During the siege people were killed by the bombs and the shelling in the most awful ways—such wounds you have no idea. Families came from other towns into Warsaw. Many people were running away. Everything was just a bloody mess.

When the Germans were finally through with the siege, they still could not enter Warsaw because there were mines under the streets and sidewalks. They moved in very slowly, and finally took over. They had a victory march with tanks in the street. I watched from a hiding place. The streets were completely empty. They marched with their goose steps and nobody was there. A dead city.

Right away the Germans started to paste up orders on the walls. Orders here, orders there. Jews immediately were not allowed to walk on the sidewalk. They could only walk freely in the ghetto. Outside the ghetto, they had to walk where the horses or cars go, in the gutter. Once, my father was on the sidewalk when some German soldier looked at him and could not believe that he was a Jew because he did not look like one. And when the soldier gave him an order to get down from the sidewalk, my father answered him, "No, I am not going. You can go." It was a Jewish section, but the soldier was not sure, and my father refused him. Then he hit my father on the face quite strongly.

Soon the Germans called everyone who had been helping Mayor Starzynski to present themselves. All my father's friends were hiding, they had disappeared. But, interestingly enough, my father said, "I am going to present myself." It was some kind of thing for him, like, let me find out what they want to do to me.

So he presented himself to the German who was the commander of the city. The commander asked for his name, and then he said, "Oh, we recognize your name. We know who you are, we know all about you. You are a very fine man." The German was an old officer, not a young one. The young ones were really the greatest Nazis. He said, "Let me shake hands with you. You are a very fine man, a very honorable man." And my father said, "I do not shake hands with the enemy." And then he said, "May I leave?" The commander said, "Yes, you may leave." And then he said, "I am very sorry for what will happen to the Jews." The German said that, knowing that my father was a Jew. But my father did not accept his hand and left.

The Germans did nothing to my father. He did not even hide anymore. He just went to the house, very sick with high blood pressure. He had problems with his heart, then he got pneumonia.

THE NAZIS TAKE OVER

After the Germans invaded Poland, the Jewish youth tried to flee to Russia. All my friends, whoever could, were running, walking, marching, riding bicycles, whatever, to Russia. The Russians and Germans had made a pact, their non-aggression treaty, and the result was to divide Poland between them. When the Germans marched on Poland from the West, the Russians marched from the East. The Russians took all of Poland east of the Bug River including the city of Lwow.

The Jews wanted to go to Russia. But, if you said you wanted to go to Russia, the Russian border guards sent you to Germany. If you said you wanted to go to Germany, they sent you to Russia. That's how the Russians were at the frontier. I know it doesn't make sense, but the Russian mind is like that. Funny things happened at the border. The Russians would take wristwatches from the Polish people coming to the borders. The Russian women were so poor they took the Polish women's nightgowns for dresses.

The Russians did not want the communists of Poland. They suspected them, did not trust them, and they put plenty of them into prison, punishing them. My uncle, Stanislaw Lubelski, was a teacher, a great communist. He took his son Tadzio and his nephew, the son of my other aunt Rosalia (Rozia), and he stayed in Lwow. He studied Russian. He was going to be the number one citizen of Russia. The Russians came in the night and sent him to Siberia without allowing him to take even coats or blankets. Just like that—a communist!

For a while his wife, my aunt, got letters. He was cold and sick. He was with the two boys, his son and his nephew.

When one went to work, the other undressed to give him his clothing. The prisoners had to share their clothes in order to go to work. If you didn't work, you didn't eat. What happened to them in Siberia, we do not know.

My uncle Lubelski was not only in the Party. He was active, a big communist, and he would do anything possible against the Polish government. He really was something. He turned all the students into communists. He was working actively, very actively, but he was very foolish because he did not realize what the result would be—although my father warned him.

I did not go to Russia because of my father. I saw everybody else was going, so I asked him what I should do. He said to me, "Now that it's a war and you are grown up, you have to decide everything for yourself. I cannot tell you anything. But in order to be safe there in Russia, you will have to answer for your father." If your father was not a worker, if he was a capitalist, his children would suffer in a Russian prison. They did not have to be political themselves.

It was dangerous to go to Russia for many reasons. Gentiles were very mistreated there because of nationalism. At that time, the Jews were treated right. They were getting jobs, they had possibilities. But not the Christian Polish people. The Polish officers who got caught had problems in Russia. In the meantime, the Ukrainian minority in Poland was killing Polish people like you kill cockroaches, they were killing the Polish soldiers and officers. They were killing Jews, too, but that's beside the point. They were killing Poles whenever they could. The Ukrainians were pro-German. You might say they were super-Nazis. They were very happy on account of this war. They figured they had a big future in Germany. I know all this from a boyfriend who went to Lwow. He became a big shot there under the Russian regime. He lost his life when the Germans attacked Russia.

One night, this boyfriend sent somebody to my house

to deliver a false card, like an embassy pass, which said I could go to Russia with him. My boyfriend wrote me a message to go with this man. All that night I could have run away. My father said, "If you want to go, this is the last moment you can do it." My father was sick, and my mother was alone taking care of him. So I decided I was not going to leave my mother, and I stayed with them.

In the meantime the Germans were beginning to establish their order in Warsaw. They immediately gave orders that the Jews would have to put on the Jewish star. The Jews wore yellow stars in Germany, but in Warsaw it was never this color: It was white with a blue Star of David that you wore on your arm. Jews wearing the arm bands could not walk safely on the streets. The Germans would hit the Jews.

In the fall of 1940 the Germans gave orders that the Jews had to move to the ghetto. Actually, there were two ghettoes. One was called the Big Ghetto, the other the Small Ghetto. I was in the Big Ghetto. There was a street connecting one to the other. But both ghettos had walls, high walls with broken bottles on top, although they had not yet been built when the Jews had to move. We did not have to move ourselves because our apartment was already in the ghetto on Nowolipie 32.

People were moving, going there to live, one family living with another. Strangers lived together. Some German Jews moved into our building. Actually, they were Polish Jews who had been living in Germany for many years and were German citizens but had been thrown out. They had to march across the frontier, thrown out by the Germans. That had already happened just before the war. The Polish government accepted them as citizens. There were all kinds of Jews in the ghetto. Every house, every nook, had some family. It was a terrible situation. So many apartments, so many houses had already been destroyed, especially in the Jewish sections.

One day, before the ghetto was closed a little later in 1940, I was walking on Marszalkowska Street, outside the ghetto, without any thought that something unusual would happen. Actually, the Jews were afraid to walk outside the ghetto. Those who wore stars would be hit by Germans passing by. But I didn't wear any star so that I could walk outside the ghetto without being beaten.

All of a sudden I saw an old admirer of mine, this Gentile fellow, who was much older than me. Years before, he had passed by my school and noticed me. He had started following me every day, wanting to make my acquaintance. He liked me. So one Sunday he had come to my father at our country house in Radosc and said, "Look, my name is so-and-so. I am a Protestant. I hope you don't mind that. Can I go out with your daughter?" My father might have been a very big Polish patriot, but his daughter had to have a Jewish husband. Diplomatically, he said, "Look, she's a young girl. She hasn't even finished school. Come back in a few years." This man then said, "I know what you mean. You don't like Gentiles." And he left. We forgot he ever existed.

All the Nazis wore leather jackets like a uniform, and there he was, wearing a shiny leather jacket with a big red *Hakenkreuz*, a swastika. I could tell he was a *Volksdeutscher*, a Pole of German descent. He was German now, not Polish anymore. When he saw me he was standing with a German pilot who was beating every Jew who passed by on the head. When he saw me, he pointed to me and started to run after me. But I knew Warsaw well enough, so I ran into one house and then out the back into a courtyard, then to another, and I disappeared. He wanted to give me up to this German who was beating Jews. That shows you how much he loved the Jews. You would never believe that someone who liked some girl would look for a chance to bring her back to be beaten.

I never put on the arm band so that I could walk about

freely and get food. I stood in lines for bread, lines for everything. I even got chocolate! I was called *débrouillarde,* which means "somebody who is resourceful" in French, somebody who runs even through fire and does not burn. I was young and everything seemed fun, as long as I didn't know what was going to happen next. All the youth who stayed, who were getting things, they were the brave ones. The older people actually did not move about. They were scared, but the young walked around and did everything. I started to sell gold.

When my father found out that I was selling gold, he could have died right then and there. He said, "Look, the police will come and I will not be able to help you. It's against the law. It's always been against the law."

Once, a thief came in my house—a big thief, a real criminal—and he came to my father and said, "You were always such a nice man. You never brought harm to anybody. You were so fair. Please accept a sack of food." He lived near us, and when he heard that my father was sick he brought him food that he had stolen from the Polish army. He said, "I will bring you any food you want." But my father did not accept it. Everybody stole at that time, but he was still living in the time of honor, of fine character, of gentlemen, and he did not realize the change. He was not stupid by any means. He was just a certain type of person.

My father worked with a Pole of German descent. He was a good Pole. During the siege of Warsaw this man got hit and his belly was torn open. My father, as sick as he was, managed to carry him on his shoulder, and he forced some people to help him get the man to the hospital. When he got him to the hospital and said his friend's German name, right away the anger was so strong against the Germans that no doctor wanted to operate on him. My father would not allow that. He said, "There is a time when you have to realize who is a traitor and who is not. He is not a traitor. He is just as good a Pole as you are." And my father forced them to operate. He simply took out his gun and said operate or else. They operated on him, so my father saved his life. When the Germans came to the Warsaw Ghetto and my father was dying, this man came to my father crying, "I want to help you. Just live, don't die." But he could not help. My father was dying anyway.

When my father was in bed sick, dying, a doctor from the pre-war Polish government came. He loved my father and he was crying. He had known my father for years, from the time of the struggle for Polish independence. They were fellow fighters. He came to help him but could not. "Look," he said to us. "He's far gone." He did not have any medicine for pneumonia, no shots—they did not have penicillin then. I knew another doctor, a Jewish doctor who happened to be a communist. Mother called him because he was one of the best lung doctors, but he gave my father medicine that caused him to bleed. When the government doctor came back, he said to my father, "This callous man should be put in prison for what he did to you!" The lung doctor had made him bleed. He did him harm so he would die faster—and without reason.

He was sick for many months until his heart gave in on the eighth of March, 1940. He was one of the last to be buried in the Jewish cemetery. His Gentile friends, his important political friends, came to his funeral. They were afraid to go where the Jews were, but they came in through the back way to pay him last respects. They spoke to my mother and told her that if he had died in normal times he would have had an orchestra and army medals. As a matter of fact, I still have my father's medal from King Carl of Romania. The other medals he had from Pilsudski had to be thrown away because they were obviously from someone involved with the government, so I could not keep them.

CAFÉ SZTUKA

Near the Tlomackie Synagogue, which was just outside the ghetto wall, there was a café that had been a Jewish restaurant before the war. It was made into a café theater by people representing Goldwyn-Mayer, and all these film distributors, movie-house owners, all these people used the café. The waitresses were all from fine families and were ladies of society. It was called Café Sztuka—*sztuka* means art—and it was at Number Two Leszno Street, where the Gertner Restaurant was before the war.

In this Café Sztuka two terrific pianists would play, Adas Goldfeder and Wladyslaw Szpilman. They played two pianos together at the same time. Goldfeder was from a very fine, aristocratic Jewish family. Szpilman played on the radio. And there also was a very famous actor, Andre Wlast. He was singing songs that said "Get out of here, get out." That's what he was singing, to get out. He never got out. There was one poet—like today in cafés where they read poetry—he was a terrific poet who looked like a Gentile. He was part Gentile, or maybe he changed faith, I don't know. Since he had some Jewish blood, he was in the ghetto. There was also a woman called Viera Gran who was a singer in nightclubs. She would sing there, and she had some sweetheart who was a baker. There were a few times the Germans came in when she was singing.

I worked there as a waitress. I got the job very quickly. The wife of one of my father's cousins was secretary of a club of actors and artists before the war and she was a partner in Café Sztuka. She gave me the job so that I could eat and bring some food home to my parents and also to my relatives.

There was one very beautiful girl, the daughter of a rabbi, who looked like a Gentile, a gorgeous blond girl. When the Germans came to the café, she would serve them. Nobody wanted to serve the Germans—we would never lower ourselves—but because she was such a beautiful look-alike Gentile girl, she would have to serve the Germans. She was not a society girl, just a real waitress. The Germans liked coming to this café. They got great satisfaction from watching the Jews, seeing how the Jews sat there and listened to the music and sang the Viennese waltzes, the *Wienervals*.

Meanwhile, the Germans were killing Jews anytime they wanted. Don't forget, the Jews were smuggling, trying to get food from the other side of the wall. The Germans would come from outside, killing, shooting. Unfortunately, there were many traitors amongst the Jews who formed a secret police working with the Gestapo. None of them was from Warsaw, I'm happy to say. They were all from Lodz, which the Germans called Litzmannstadt. They were all intelligentsia—doctors, engineers, police—none of them uneducated or from the lower classes. They were all professionals—and disgustingly mean. We were afraid of them like fire. Their headquarters were on the same street as Café Sztuka, but on the other side. The building was Number Thirteen Leszno Street. Because of that, they were called Number Thirteens.

This was the Jewish Gestapo against the Jews. They had green bands on their caps. The regular Jewish police had blue bands. This Jewish Gestapo would come into the café, but we did not like to serve them. They did a lot of the dirty work. Let's say some Jews had hidden in their apartments dollars or money or gold that they could sell to buy food. The Jewish Gestapo would give away all these secrets to the

Germans. And the Germans would come shooting and killing. There was not mass killing yet. It was just bad treatment, very awful treatment, but not mass exterminations.

When I worked in the café, I had to wear a black dress and high heels. Once, I was coming home very tired when suddenly the Germans came with a few cameras taking pictures of me on the streets like, "Look how they live in the ghetto. The Jews who work wear elegant high-heeled shoes." Of course, it was my job always to look dressed up. But the reality was not this film the Germans took. There were people lying on the sidewalks without food, swollen and dying. There was typhus. There were cadavers all over, their skin bursting open. They looked like lepers. They were covered with papers, smelling. Rats were eating them.

Some German Jews were given jobs outside the walls of the Warsaw Ghetto. They would go to work in the morning, and in the evening they would come back through the wall. They were called *placowka*—*placowka* was the name for factories outside the ghetto, on the Aryan side, and for the work units who would leave the ghetto to work and then return. One day these German Jews were marching off to work past the SS men on guard. These German Jews were all raising their hands, hollering, *"Heil Hitler!"* and the SS men did not even answer them, did not look at them, did not even spit at them. In Warsaw, we just laughed when these German Jews screamed, *"Heil Hitler!"*—as if Hitler would help them—this was the funniest part. This really made us laugh in this tragic time.

I found out later that when there was an action against the Jews, these German Jews were killed first. All of them looked like Gentiles; they were of mixed blood. Because there was this racial business—if the mother or father or grandfather or great-grandfather was a Jew, you were a Jew. But there were many of them who did not even know what it meant to be a Jew.

Jews were starving, even though food was being smuggled in. We did not have food, but we could get smuggled-in strawberries on the street. I remember one day I bought myself all kinds of goodies. I was walking on the street and a man came and he grabbed all the food and ran away.

There was one man who would walk the streets singing in bad Polish, Jewish Polish, "*Oy, te bony, ja chce zyc jak ony.* Oy, the bones, I want to live like others." We were getting food cards. If you got enough of these cards you could eat. If you did not, you died. He wanted to eat the same as everybody else—although nobody was eating that well. It was a starvation ghetto. This man sang his songs walking completely nude, summer or winter.

The conditions in the ghetto were so terrible, you have no idea. People hated each other. You understand, they were starving. They could kill each other for food. We had a family from Lodz in our apartment. My mother cooked. The wife of this man came and ate up my mother's soup, so my mother complained to me. The man did not like my mother complaining, so he pushed her around and beat her up. When I came home from work that day I hit him on the head with an iron pot. I got even for my mother. He got no pity from me. He never touched her anymore.

I did not see any resistance leaflets or newspapers in the ghetto. If I ever saw any resistance, any writing on the walls, it was in the Aryan section. There they would write on the walls things like "Only pigs go to the movies," because going to the movies helped the Germans by making people forget about the war, forget about resisting. But in the ghetto we were only worried about food, the cold, the sickness and the lice. We were completely demoralized.

We were so demoralized that people became disrespectful of each other. If a married man had a sweetheart, he brought her to his house, and the wife was lucky if he did not throw her out on the street. If he gave his wife food and a place to sleep on the floor, she was considered lucky. The youth thought only how to grab and to survive, nothing else. They only talked about England: "England will never come, they are false, they are no good." Before the war Poland had a pact with France and England that they would help Poland in case of attack, but they did nothing.

Once I found a child who was alone, starving and cold. I was so sorry for this child that I took him to Janusz Korczak, a writer who ran a school for orphans. He was really doing a marvelous job with them. I think they were getting some money from America through certain channels, and they were getting food. So I did everything possible to bring the child to this school. I thought it was a beautiful thing to do at the time. I was so proud of myself for having arranged it. Later, during an action, Korczak and everyone in his school were taken to be killed. Sure enough, this child went together with the other children of Korczak to die. I did not mean for him to die. If I had known that was going to happen ...

One day, papers snowed down announcing, "Now is the end of the Jews." We got this paper and did not know what it was about. Such a fear in the whole ghetto. Where is America? Where is England? They were supposed to march, but they are still not here? What will be? We did not know what would happen next. But we already had the first signs. German jeeps were going through the streets, shooting into crowds at random. That's how they started the actual killing of the Jews.

I still had a job at Café Sztuka, and I would go to work because I had to bring food home. One day, some Germans came into the café, officers with the big *Hakenkreuz,* and they just went after me. I had a hairstyle with braids around my head, and I was very beautiful and young. One German came over to me. He looked at me and shook his head and started to laugh. He said a German expression, *"Quatsch mit*

Soße," which means "zero," or "you are finished." He had the pleasure of seeing a beautiful girl and scaring her. I did not understand German, but I remembered that. "You are a nobody."

After the Germans left, all the waitresses, these ladies, they were crying. There was one woman in particular, the wife of a lawyer, who was crying, saying, "What will we do with the children? They will kill all the children. All the children! From the smallest they will take them." She was crying. "How will we hide them? What are we supposed to do?" And we just talked and talked without sense—helpless.

"WE WILL MEET IN THE OTHER WORLD"

Soon, there were roundups all the time, every day. Germans would come in the morning, shooting in the air, hollering, *"Da runter!"* Everybody had to come down from their apartments. Then the Germans put them together and took them to the *Umschlagplatz,* the train station, where they were loaded into the animal train to Majdonek or Treblinka, to the gas chambers. We still did not know that we were going to be sent to our deaths. As a matter of fact, they were telling us that we were going to work in a camp. I did not know what was really happening to the Jews once they left on the trains. Only when I got to America after the war did I learn about the gassing.

One of my cousins was also named Zosia, Zosia Strumfeld Cohn. Zosia was a pianist, a painter, the wife of a lawyer, and she had a little child named Ryzio. She saw a sign on the wall that said if you go to the train station, you will get a big loaf of bread with marmalade. Zosia, that big smart girl, took her husband and she went to be killed without even realizing it, without even trying to run.

I did not have for a moment the idea of staying and waiting to give myself up. I would run. But I continued living at home as long as I could because there was a bed, everything. My mother would stay in the house while I was the fighter, always looking for food, for a place to run to, a place to hide. My mother did not believe what would happen. She thought I was nuts.

I kept on thinking about escaping, about crossing over to the Aryan side. But how to get out, I had no idea. I had heard that people were escaping through the cemetery. But how to get to the cemetery when there were so many police, so many Germans, I did not know.

One day, I got very friendly with a girl, Franka, and I said we should go together. Remember that the German Jews left the ghetto to work and came back to sleep. These went as *placowka,* work squads. So I decided I would go out with some *placowka,* as these Jews who left the ghetto each day to work were called. I would see if I could go out with the *placowka* and come back. It would be an experiment. If I could do this, I would bring my mother the next day and we would go out but not return.

Then I heard that at the exit from the ghetto on Leszno and Zelazna Streets there was one German guard who would pretend he did not see what was going on if you gave him silver coins. So I took some coins that I hid in my pants and went with this girl and tried to go out along with the *placowka.* I gave the German this silver, and he pretended he was checking our papers. He did all right. He smiled. He got his money and pocketed it. But just when I was supposed to go out, there was an action at the Toebbens clothing factory, which was on the corner of Zelazna and Leszno. There was shooting and killing and we had to run away.

But who did I run into on the corner of the street? None other than my cousin on my mother's side, Janek Mikicinski, a boy of excellent character. Janek was now a Jewish policeman, but he was a communist and the Party was helping him. He said, "Zosia, what are you doing here? Are you crazy? The biggest roundup is going on here. If they catch you now, you are finished. Run away from here, and run fast!" As soon as he finished talking there was more shooting and killing. I ran over ruins, running, falling, and getting up again until I got back to my mother. I was dirty, my clothing torn. I had lost a shoe, but I made it back to my mother.

I still did not know how to get out. My boyfriend,

Janek Pinczewski, offered to help me. He had been a boy-friend I cared for a lot, but my cousin, Janka Lubelska, took him away from me. I had gotten her a job in another café. She was very stupid. Her mother said to her, "You better take that boyfriend away from Zosia." He was a young boy. He liked her and I was sick at the time with a terrific cold. So he took her home and they started to flirt.

Janka was the daughter of the communist Stanislaw and Mania Lubelski. She became a policewoman at the Pawiak Street prison, where those people who were to leave Poland because they had foreign passports were kept. She was a policewoman, but she was faking, giving the prisoners food, bringing them letters, information, and so on.

So I met this boyfriend, Janek Pinczewski, on the street. He said to me, "You know what, Zosia? We'll run away together to the Aryan section."

"What about my mother?" I asked.

"We'll take her, too."

He was a young fellow but was not energetic. He was not capable of doing much for himself. He said he had an uncle who was on the Aryan side who had an apartment. We would go there and disappear and finish with this ghetto.

Should I or shouldn't I? I made up my mind very fast. First of all, he was not faithful to me. He was never faithful. If he was not faithful in love, he would not be faithful for more important matters like life and death. This type of fel-low I did not need. So I said to him, "Give me your hand." And I sang to him a song that was popular at that time about how we will meet in the other world.

"What are you talking about? I want to take you to the Aryan section."

"You go to your uncle. Goodbye."

He went left, I went right. All of a sudden there was a big action. The Germans almost caught us there. There was so much beating and shooting. But I ran through it like running through a fire and nothing happened to me. It was the second time this had happened. My mother stayed at home peacefully while I ran through fire.

But I still had to do something, we had to leave the ghetto. But how?

THE END OF
THE FAMILY

In one day I lost my father's family, I lost them all. My father, of course, had already died, but he had four sisters and their families. Three of my aunts had moved from their apartments and lived together at Leszno 42. This apartment had an opening through the ceiling to the roof that was eventually camouflaged and would become a refuge. We could go to the roof and from the roof to other houses and run away. I considered this to be a good apartment because it had that hidden door.

My mother was in love with my father's family. She wanted us to do everything for them. "You must put them together and take care of them, all of us," she said. It was a bit hard on me. I would visit them with my mother and we would all sleep on the floor. There were men and women and a lot of children, and nobody was doing anything, just waiting for me to help them. What they did was to come to me: "Zosia, what will we do? Get us papers, the Life Cards."

Since they spoke Polish so beautifully, without any Jewish accent, and because they looked like Gentiles, they could have saved themselves by going to the Aryan section. They could have found a way. They were not doing well at all, but they were not completely without money. They could have managed. If somebody is desperate, he can do anything. He has to save himself, even if he goes without a penny. But they did not have any courage. They could have gone amongst Gentiles even without money. Anybody would have opened their doors for them; they would have taken them for Gentiles for sure. But they did not even try.

Of all my aunts, I loved Rozia Warszawska the most. She was the nicest, had the best character. Her husband Ludwik died in Leszno 42 of starvation. One of their sons, Zygmunt Warszawski, had married a girl named Wanda Mundlak, and they were trying to survive on their own. The communist Stanislaw Lubelski had taken Rozia's other son, Rysio, to Lwow, to the Russian side, from where they were sent to Siberia, as I mentioned. Rozia died of heartache as a result; she just gave up and died. Another aunt, Stanislaw Lubelski's wife, Mania, was there in Leszno 42 with her daughter, Janka. (Remember, Mania's son Tadzio was also with his father in Siberia.) A third aunt, Anka, and her husband, Adolf Korentajer, and their two daughters, Stella and Janka, lived there as well, along with another relative, Mania Zeidlitz.

There was also my oldest aunt, Severina Strumfeld, but she did not live at Leszno 42. Severina looked almost exactly like my sister, Roma, except prettier. She had a beautiful nose, very blue eyes, golden hair, a beautiful crown of braids around her head. With glasses on a golden chain around her neck, she was a beautiful woman, an aristocrat.

She lived with Hela, her middle daughter, who was a communist, as I mentioned before. Her oldest daughter, also named Zosia, was taken by the Germans on the train with her son and her husband, a lawyer. Zosia was the foolish one who went to the trains because the Germans said she would get bread with marmalade. The youngest daughter of Severina, Irena (Irka), was in France studying engineering at Toulouse.

Severina fell somewhere and broke her hip. Since she was in her sixties, she was in bed all the time and could not move. There was an action, a roundup in front of their house. The Germans were catching Jews and everybody was running away. But she could not move. She stayed in bed while her daughter, Hela, hid between the clothing in the closet. That's how Hela knew the way her mother lost her life. The German came and said, "My poor dear mother, you look just like my mother. I will not let you suffer." Then he took out his gun and shot her in the head. The German killed her right in bed.

If you call that pity or heart, maybe it was. The German knew how she would lose her life. However, it was a dreadful thing. The whole brain went all over the bed. But the German did not see Hela. She went out later and came and found us.

Hela's younger sister, Irka, as I said, was studying in France. She almost married a Chinese fellow. She had fallen in love, but when she came back to visit the family on vacation before the war they discouraged her from marrying. Then she met a White Russian, a prince or something, who was an engineer studying with her. They got married. He was a Gentile, but because she was Jewish they were sent to Drancy, a concentration camp near Paris. From there they were sent to Germany. After the war, when I got to France, I went to the police looking for Irka. I found her last address, and they said she was taken to Drancy and she never came back. There were no signs of her. Maybe she survived, maybe not. She just disappeared, another unknown ...

One day the Germans encircled the house at Leszno 42, and they called everybody down. I was with my mother and we were sleeping on the floor with my aunts and we were supposed to go down with them. Instead, I ran upstairs to Bolek, a young fellow who was a friend of mine. He knew many of the Jewish police and he spoke Russian, so I said to him, "Go down and see what you can do." Along with the German Nazis, there were Ukrainians, Lithuanians, Latvians, and Jewish police.

"Try to get all the family out," I told Bolek. They were already forming lines to march to the trains at the *Umschlag-*

platz. So he came back and said, "I saw Marian. He's in the police. I'll see what he can do." But Marian, my ex-husband, the one I had married and divorced before the war, simply washed his hands of us and turned away. "Well," he said, "too bad. Zosia is there with her family. Too bad." He did not lift a finger to help. From that moment I had plenty of hate for him, believe me.

Then Bolek tried to talk to a Ukrainian who understood his Russian. He made up a story that my mother was his mother and I was his sister. He said our family was dead. Maybe because Bolek spoke Russian to him, which is close to Ukrainian, he felt sympathetic. I don't know why, maybe it was just luck, but the Ukrainian said you can take out your mother and sister from the line, but nobody else. Everybody else had to stay.

So I said to Bolek, "Look, if you cannot take out the rest now, maybe you can still try." "Impossible!" he said. I begged him. I told him I would give him something, a lot of money. Nothing doing. "But you know a policeman who knows some people at the *Umschlagplatz.* You have to get them out of there!" "All right," he agreed. "Let's go."

Then Janka, the daughter of my aunt Anka Korentajer, came over to me and she gripped my knees, kneeling on the ground, begging me to take her with me. "Zosia, help me, save me, please. Don't leave us here." I had to pull her hands away. I could not even cry. I just walked away with my mother, that's all. I had to make my choice. I will never forget this moment till my dying day, how I left all of my family, Janka especially, and I never saw them again.

I could not get back to the *Umschlagplatz,* but Bolek did, as he promised. He spent hours screaming, hollering, calling their names, "Lubelska! Korentajer! Anka! Mania! Janka! Stella!" But nobody answered. What must have happened is that they were so afraid they went into some corner. There were thousands of people and they must have put themselves someplace where they could not hear. They were afraid, and they were put on the train. If Bolek had seen them, he would have gotten them out by force.

Only Mania Lubelska, the wife of the professor, escaped. She went to the back of the line with her daughter, Janka. When they were marching to the *Umschlagplatz,* they cut out of the line and ran away. So they came back. I saw them a couple of times more, but then I lost contact with them.

On my mother's side of the family there were cousins. My mother's mother's sister was Telca Trauman and she had two children, Lutek and Franka. Her son Lutek was married to Hela, and before the war they had a store that was just outside the Small Ghetto. A Gentile woman who used to be a saleswoman took over the store from them. They lived in the Small Ghetto and managed to get out. Lutek and Hela went through the wall to live in the Aryan section. They took their daughter Hanka and lived with his mother Telca. His sister Franka also lived there, and brought her daughter Bronia.

Telca made believe she was deaf and mute in order to hide her Jewish accent. She had blue eyes, a good face. Some Germans stationed nearby brought her food, everything, to help this family, figuring that they were helping Gentiles. And they got through the war this way to die natural deaths. Bronia's father, Adolf, was taken away one day near the *Umschlagplatz* and killed, but Franka and her mother, Telca, were able to get some kind of papers and hide in the apartment in the Aryan section. Lutek Trauman was stopped one day, the Germans pulled his pants down, and when they saw that he was circumcised, they killed him on the spot.

Soon after they got to the Aryan side Bronia was put in a Catholic convent. She was five years old, and she was told by a priest, "You are a Jewish girl, but now you are a Christian, and never say anything. After the war you can be

Jewish again." But Bronia after the war did not want to be Jewish anymore and she remained Catholic. After all the suffering, her mother, Franka, was driven out of her mind because her daughter remained a Christian. Bronia is still in Poland, while Hela and her daughter Hanka moved to Israel.

Janek Mikicinski, the Jewish policeman who told me to run from the action at Leszno and Zelazna, and his sister Wanda were the children of another sister of my mother's mother. Mikicinski was not their original name. The family went to Russia before the revolution, and they changed their name to sound Gentile. But their father was killed by bandits, and they returned to Poland. Wanda and Janek had a Gentile nanny when they were children, and this nanny hid Wanda and a friend of hers throughout the war. Janek was killed, but Wanda survived and moved to Israel.

There were others. The Plywaks were the poorest relations of my mother. He was just a poor barber who could hardly make a living before the war, and he died with his wife of hunger. They got swollen like all the others who were lying on the streets, dying.

They had two daughters, Cesia and Marysia, who had lived with us when my father was still alive. It was very difficult for us to feed them and take care of them. One day, both Cesia, who was very courageous, and Marysia said they were going to run away to the Aryan section. I do not know what happened to them. But I heard through somebody that they were caught amongst the Gentiles. That's how they disappeared.

And that's the end of the family.

"MAY YOU DIE
AMONGST THE *GOYIM*"

Soon after my father's family was taken from Leszno 42, I talked with a man in our building on Nowolipie 32 who had a marmalade factory outside of the ghetto. His name was Pawel Gombinski. Maybe he was collaborating—so many were. You never knew—it could be your best friend. Anyway, Pawel said to me, "Zosia, I can tell you one thing. Tonight or tomorrow morning our house will go, everyone will disappear." He knew, and it was so.

I started to prepare. I took all my father's papers. He used to keep a family tree to know from what town, what century, our relatives came. He loved that family tree, but I tore it to bits. I had my baccalaureate, my graduation certificate, and I tore it up. The name Goldberg should disappear. Photos of all the family I tore up, everything. Only one baby photo of my nephew Ronald in America, a picture of my father, because he did not look like a Jew, and the medal from the King of Romania—I hid them all in my brassiere for four years. And I kept one bracelet, a silver bracelet my father gave me when I finished school, a bracelet with Eastern elements, like Arab camels, which would become very important later on in Germany. I tore up my mother's pictures completely, the pictures of my sister Roma, the cousins, everybody.

Earlier, soon after the ghetto was closed off from the rest of Warsaw, the Germans said we had to hand in radios and all furs. They were just filling up on the wealth of the Jews for their soldiers and their families back in Germany. I turned in the radio just to have a paper proving that I did, but I destroyed it before giving it to them—there was only powder inside; it was a box of powder, nothing else. The fur I sold.

That night I took an axe and destroyed the rest of the furniture and our belongings. I took two sacks and stuffed in cushions, blankets, jackets, whatever I could. I told my mother to put on all the underwear, all the dresses, the jackets, whatever she could. We were so fat and so big, and it was very hot. It was late Fall, but the weather was very hot.

I did not ask anybody what to do. I was all on my own. Whenever I did something, I never asked anybody. I never asked if I should go to the left or the right. It was by intuition. Besides, you couldn't talk to anybody. You did not know who was a traitor. I was too afraid.

It was around twelve o'clock at night. I was all dressed up waiting because the neighbor had said we would be taken that night or the next morning. All of a sudden I heard downstairs in the courtyard all the Jews talking, a very big noise. I went downstairs. There was a Jew with a big beard who I had never seen before, and I went over to him and asked, "What's happening? Could you tell me?" I could not speak Yiddish, so I spoke Polish to him. I think he understood me, but he got very angry that I did not speak Yiddish, so he spat at me, *"Du solst starben zwischem goyim!"*

I did not understand exactly what he said, so I went back to my apartment and repeated it to my mother. "What does *'Du solst starben zwischem goyim'* mean?" She said, "Who cursed you like this?" She explained to me that he had said, "May you die amongst the *goyim!*" He said this because if you did not speak Yiddish, you were an outcast. I said to myself, "Wait a minute. This is not a curse. God spoke through his mouth! From now on, no matter what we do, we don't stay amongst Jews. We go to the *goyim.* We'll run away from the ghetto!" This Jew made it clear: I will not stay with them for anything in this world. Amongst the Jews it is sure death, but with the Gentiles, it is only possible death. I will try that!

Not only did it seem impossible to get to the Aryan side, but once there you would have no place to go. No bed, no home. Do you know what it meant, to sleep on the sidewalk or in the stairways? You could not sleep on the street because they could pick you up. Any Gentile could call a German and say, "She's a Jewess!" I was afraid. I could not make such a move easily. I did not know how, not yet, but I did know that we had to get out of the ghetto.

Meanwhile, we had to escape from our building. Near our house there was a velodrome where racing bicycles were sold. There was a hole in the wall of the velodrome from the siege of Warsaw that led to other streets. I started thinking. If anything happened I would go through that hole to another street and run away.

About three or four o'clock that morning I said to my mother, "We are going. We are leaving the house, never to come back." As a matter of fact, I even broke the windows. Everything I broke so the Germans could never carry out any actions from there.

My mother said, "You're crazy!" She was about forty-five years old, not an old woman. But all the older people had the same way of thinking. The old ones wanted to stay in the houses. They did not realize that the next morning, or three days later, they would be taken and killed. They wanted to stay in their homes. Only the youth ran. When I told my mother that I would go out into the streets, she was very upset.

She was cooking a big pot of *krupnik,* barley soup. I said to her, you cannot go with *krupnik* because this is hot. I had a lot of difficulty with her. I had to carry these two sacks. So, early in the morning, we ran to the hole. My mother could not go through, she was too clumsy with all the clothing she had on. So I pushed her through the hole in the wall. Then I pushed myself through. I took the sacks, and she took the soup pot. When we climbed out on the other side we were on Nowolipki Street. We were still in the ghetto, but now we were homeless and on the run.

When we got there my mother said, "You did a good thing. Now we are on the street. You are a good daughter. Now what do we do?" She was sarcastic, but I said, "Keep quiet and don't talk, we have to listen." Sure enough, there was shooting, screaming, Germans hollering, *"Da runter! Da runter!"* and the whole house was finished. They were taking them away, or killing whoever was resisting on the spot. Then there was great silence. I never again saw those people, those neighbors. Once, later, when I was living in the Aryan section, I saw one woman, a Gentile, a neighbor who used to live in our building before the ghetto was formed. She recognized me, but she made believe that she didn't see me. She could have turned me in, yet she didn't. But the other neighbors ... I never saw them again.

THE BRUSHMAKERS' FACTORY

We were on the street. I was breaking my head, thinking. My mother was breaking my head, too. "Where do we go now? Do you want to sleep on the street?"

"Well," I said, "we will knock on somebody's door. They will let us in." We knocked and I said, "We ran away from Nowolipie Street. Will you please let us in?" They shut the door in our faces.

There was a brushmakers' factory that made brushes for the Gestapo. That does not mean they were collaborating with the Gestapo. In all the factories the Jews were paying the Gestapo huge amounts of money to keep us alive, to give us work, because they did not even want to give us work. Actually, the Gestapo fought with the SS because they wanted our money. They did not want to give us to the SS right away. They wanted first to squeeze us for money, then, when they were finished with us, they would give us away.

So I was thinking about this brushmakers' factory on Franciszkanska Street. I always knew somebody, some young fellow. I'd say, "How are you? You know you have to help me." Remember, I was beautiful and very young. So wherever I went they were always opening doors for me. I had this kind of luck. Wherever I went, I found help. I went to the right places, too.

So we were there, at the brushmakers' factory. The Germans came through, checking. We slept on the floor. We pretended we worked there. Everyone was pretending. No one was really working, just doing the minimum, just enough to look like we were working. I was doing work for myself and for my mother because she could not work fast enough. So I had to make brushes for the both of us.

I was walking on Franciszkanska Street one day with my mother when I saw my aunt Mindla. Since my mother's mother had died early, her father, my grandfather, had married another woman, and together they had three daughters, Mindla, Henia, and Bajla. They were half sisters to my mother. Mindla was very beautiful. And there she was with all her children—the Jewish police taking Mindla and all the children in a pushcart to the station. At that time I did not know what happened to Jews who went to the *Umschlagplatz*. I did not know they were taking them to their deaths. It was very vague still, but I knew it could not be good.

I went to the policeman and said, "Look, she's my aunt. Leave her alone." "Who are you to tell me?" he said. "What do you mean? *You* get on the pushcart." And he picked me up and put me on the pushcart. My mother was there too, and I was in despair that my mother would be taken. She would be taken in a second without my help. Then came another Jewish policeman who knew me very well. He said, "Are you crazy? That's Zosia. Leave her alone." "All right," the first policeman said. "Let her get out." And they took away Mindla and her children. She was crying, begging, "Zosia, help!" What could I do? I could do nothing. I tried. I will never forget her face, how they took her with her three children. She was so beautiful, that woman. But she had a Jewish accent, Jewish everything, and she could not help herself. Henia and Bajla went somewhere, to Wilno, then maybe to Russia. I never knew what happened to them.

Then they moved the brush factory to Swietojerska Street, to a big courtyard. By this courtyard was Ogrod Krasinski, a big garden, a very important spot where the religious people used to gather but which was now on the other side of the ghetto. When the factory moved, we went to live in a building with maybe eight or ten apartments. We took over one apartment. I just opened the door and went in. Our apartment had beautiful paintings, silver, the most

43

expensive linen. It was the apartment of some very wealthy family who had run away, or maybe they were dead. I had one room with my mother, and in the same room was another bed for a friend of mine from the Café Sztuka, Helena Goldberg, along with her husband and mother-in-law, Stefa Goldberg, who had the same name as my mother, but they were not relations. My mother had known Stefa Goldberg as a young girl. We were all living together.

Helena was the daughter of one of these filmmakers or producers from Café Sztuka. She went with a lot of men. She had a husband, but he meant nothing to her, even though he was a Jewish policeman in the ghetto. She did whatever she wanted. She was sex-crazy more than anything else. She was so sure, since her husband was a policeman and she knew all these brushmakers, that she would be safe. Then one day they put her on the line for death and they took her to the *Umschlagplatz*. Nobody helped her. She went right to the station. She disappeared, this girl, and when I returned to the apartment I was left with her husband and mother-in-law.

In another room of the apartment there were families from Number Thirteen Leszno Street, the Jewish Gestapo headquarters. They would eat the most fancy stuff you could imagine, all smuggled. Their brothers, sisters, and husbands were all working for the Germans. They had a good time. They were not scared or anything. They were sure they would be saved.

I continued working at the brushmakers' factory. I was always looking for a possible chance to run away from the ghetto, thinking what could or could not be done. We were making big brushes for cleaning the streets. I had to make a really large quantity for my mother as well as for myself.

The head of our brushmakers was a Jew from Lodz. He was an engineer, and he was working with one Gentile fellow, Kudasiewicz, a wonderful person. He really helped me a lot. There was another fellow there who was Ukrainian. These three ran the factory for the Gestapo.

Meanwhile, the Germans came, rounding people up every day. One day they said, "Everyone who is a redhead will go." Then the next day, "Everyone who is freckled." Another day, those with kinky hair; another, those with the Jewish nose; another, those who look like Gentiles; another, those who look beautiful. Then, those who are ugly, those with bow legs. Too old. All pregnant women. All women with little children. All men. Every day there was something else.

On one particularly terrible day they said whoever is over forty will go. My father had prepared Polish passports for us, just in case. So I falsified the passport, making it out that my mother was thirty-three years old. My own age I left, since it did not matter. Then I painted her face, braided her hair around her head. When I think how she looked, like an idiot, not young but grotesque, the way I fixed her up! And I combed my hair in this à la Gretchen style, a German hairstyle.

Then the Germans started making their selections. I was trying to find out which was the good side. When they said left, you had to go left. When they said right, you had to go right. I was asking here, asking there. Then I saw a policeman, Szymek Katz, who was one of my friends. Some say he was collaborating, but he was a fine fellow. He was not really collaborating. It was pretend work more than anything else. "So, Szymek," I said, "tell me which side." He showed me with his eyes.

Then I put my mother in front of me to see where she went, so I could push her into the right line if I needed to. Naturally there was a big fat man, a German from the SS with a leather stick, and he hit my mother to be selected for death. I ran out from the line without saying one word. I grabbed her by the coat and I kicked her into the crowd of people for life, for work. Then I stood straight like a soldier. Let them decide what they wanted. They were paralyzed. They had never seen anything like it, the *chutzpa* to take someone out from the death line and push her back to life! And there I was standing at attention.

There was a German doctor, an officer from the army. He was standing next to the SS man, although he was not SS. This SS man was the one who saw that the work was done. He was not killing or anything. So this fatso SS asked the doctor, "What should I do with her?" The doctor said, "Let her go, let her go." So I went to my mother.

We were standing, forming six or eight lines, when all of a sudden I saw one of the Ukrainians who was helping the Germans leaning out a window on the fourth or fifth floor. He asked what he should do with the child he held in his hands. The child was about nine or ten years old. *"Da runter!"* a German shouted, meaning that he should throw him out the window. And he threw him out. The boy was smashed to bits on the street while all the Jews in the lines were standing and looking. Not one word, not one cry came from anybody, as if we were all paralyzed. There was a silence, that's all …

A few days before, I had found a little child in some rags, abandoned in one of the apartments of the brushmakers' compound. He looked green, and he had such an old face, completely old. That's how the Jewish children looked, even when they were very young. I wanted to take care of him. My mother asked, "How can you take care of him? You will be taken." I had to leave the child. I found in one corner of the courtyard a little doghouse. There was a little baby chained to that doghouse with a dish of water, so I put the child there. If they crawled to the dish, they would be able to drink the water …

When the Germans were finished with their selection from the lines, we went back to work and then back to our house. I had already had enough of this selection to the right and to the left, and I was really exhausted. I just lost my spirit and I said to my mother, "Maybe we should go to sleep like some of the others, take poison and it would be the end." But as much as my mother was not really grasping the tragedy and why I was running and hiding and trying to do one thing and the other just to get away from being sent to the trains, she said, "Oh, no, we are alive and we have to live, there is no such thing as killing oneself." She didn't allow me, and so I stopped that way of thinking.

LIFE CARD

One day I learned from a Number Thirteen I knew that the Germans were coming. Something told me that this time, for this selection, I should not keep my mother with me, that I better hide her.

There was another group collaborating with the Germans besides these Number Thirteens, a group they called *Pogotowie,* which means paramedics in English. They picked up the dead bodies and cleaned the streets, but they also collaborated with the Germans, turning people in. So I went over to one of the *Pogotowie,* and I said, "Look, you are so sweet, you are so charming, you are so beautiful. As a matter of fact, I don't know why we haven't gotten closer to each other." I flirted with him because I had a purpose. "Look, could you take my mother with your family for tomorrow?" They lived in a building where they were hiding their families. I asked if my mother could go there.

"Oh, yes, why not? I'll take her."

"Do you promise that you will save her?"

"I swear to God. You can be sure."

So the next day they took her. My mother did not want to go. "Don't give me away to them," she said. "They will kill me."

"Go with them," I said. "You have to take a chance. Today I feel something will go wrong."

People were hiding all the time. They hid behind walls that were completely covered, cemented, and painted over by others on the outside. When the action was over the wall was knocked down. If the people who had built the wall were killed, the people inside the wall would never get out. That was the chance they took when they hid behind walls.

So my mother went to the building where the *Pogotowie* lived, and I went through the selection. They did nothing to me because I looked like a good worker for them. At the end of the day I looked for my mother but could not find her. Finally, I don't know how, she came back, shaking, in awful condition. She had grown older just from fear. This woman in the other family would not let her in, but somehow my mother survived and came back.

After every selection the Germans gave what they called a Life Card, a document that meant you could live and work. Now I had a Life Card, but my mother did not because she had not gone to the selection. At the next selection, you had to show the Life Card you received from the last selection; you had to show you had a right to be in this part of the ghetto. So I went over to the manager of our brush factory and I said to him, "Look, do me a favor. Falsify one card. Make me one card."

"Why, what use is it to you?"

"Make me one card for my mother. I have mine, but I need one for her."

So he said to me, "Ten thousand dollars—if you have ten thousand dollars you get a Life Card."

"What do you mean, ten thousand dollars? You know damn well this is good for one day, maybe for two days!" And he started to laugh, "Ten thousand dollars!"

I had good nails, so I took him and started to scratch his face. That's what he got for those ten thousand dollars. While this was happening, a little German soldier came over, an ordinary soldier, and he asked me, "Why are you beating him up?"

I could not speak a word of German, so he called over another Jew to translate what I was saying. I told him the truth. I had asked the manager for a Life Card, and he would not give it to me unless I gave him ten thousand dollars. So the soldier said, *"Verflucht!* Come with me!" He went into the office, and with his big boots he kicked the doors open, took a card and said, "Here it is."

And so, my mother was safe, at least until the next selection.

From now on I had a friend. Every time I went out, the German soldier would call to me. He knew I did not speak German. He gave me bread every morning. He was an old German, an old man. He did say one thing that I could understand, that he was against the Nazis. He had nothing against the Jews. He had nothing against anybody. He had probably been in Poland during the First World War. He was just a man in the army, and he saw what was happening to the Jews. He could not stand it.

The roundups continued. My mother and I made it through several more selections. Then came the day the Germans said they were taking all the brushmakers to the *Umschlagplatz* for a selection. I went to this German, and I tried to ask him what kind of selection it would be. He called somebody over to translate. So I asked him. "What do we need?" He said, "Water and no baggage. Don't bring any clothing, nothing else."

"Water and nothing else"—I understood this to be the end.

I was with my friend, Eli, from Lodz, and Szymek Katz. We went out into the streets, heading for the *Umschlagplatz.* The streets were all empty, no people, just ruins and empty houses, and here or there some factories. All three of us had our mothers with us; we were caring for our mothers, trying to save them. Hardly anyone else was. Children were not trying to save their parents. Parents were ballast for them, just like little children were ballast to the women. If a pregnant woman could cut her belly, she would do so in order not to be pregnant. I asked Eli where they were taking us, what would happen. "Don't worry," he said, "nothing will happen." Then I saw the *Umschlagplatz,* the little train depot, and I saw the cattle train.

On the other side of the *Umschlagplatz* were houses. In one house I knew that my friend Lolek Rubinstein, a musician from Lodz, was working for the Germans, making the papers, putting the names on the Life Cards. So I left my mother with Eli and Szymek. I knocked on the window. I said, "Lolek, get me a card! Throw me a card, and one for my mother too!"

He said, "I haven't found yours yet. I'll find it. Don't worry."

But while I was talking, I felt something like a pin in my back. A German SS man saw me and put a bayonet in my back, not enough to wound me, just enough to scare me, to play with me. *"Raus!"* So I moved away, but when I saw that the SS man was gone, I went back to the window. But then the SS man came back again, and this time he pushed me harder with his bayonet, so I had to leave.

Then I remembered somebody else I knew who had cards who was also in the crowd at the *Umschlagplatz.* So I went to him, and I made up some story, a lie. I asked him to look. He knew me, and he trusted me because he knew my mother and father, my family. He did not think that I would lie to him. But I did because I said to myself: by hook or by crook we have to save ourselves. I got the cards. Unfortunately, they were in a different name, but I didn't care. I didn't care about anybody anymore. I had to save myself. Right there was the *Umschlagplatz,* no place to run. There were the SS soldiers, the guards. I was in such despair that I had played this trick, and I disappeared into the crowd. But I could not live with this trick. I could not stand it. I went back and returned the cards. And so I still did not have the cards I needed, and I didn't know what to do.

While I was trying to get a Life Card, the cattle trains were slowly filling up. At one point the SS got a young girl. I remember only her first name, Marysia. She was known as a fantastic singer, a beautiful voice, and the Jewish policemen tried to save her from getting on the train, so they told the SS men how beautifully she could sing. An SS man stopped her and told her to sing "Ave Maria." She began to sing, and it was great, something beautiful even in that chaos. When she finished, the SS man pushed her onto the train. Just like that. How ridiculous to think that her singing could save her from the fate of all the other Jews.

We were waiting there all day, and people were already being pushed to the train. It became night. We could no longer sleep in the apartment. We came across a pushcart, and we slept there that night. My mother was sleeping on top of the pushcart, and I was sleeping under it with Szymek and Eli. Eli also had his fiancée. They were in love, and he had a little child he had found. He carried this child in a valise, keeping it with him all the time, trying to save it. He injected the child with something so it would not cry and made a hole in the valise so that the child could breathe. Eli was taking care of his own mother as well.

All that night I shook and cried. My mother said, "Why don't you sleep? What's the matter with you? You are so crazy, I don't know what to say. You are just nervous." I had gotten one card made, and it was in my name. Jews, friends of mine, made the card illegally. They made the card in my name because I was the younger one so I should survive. They could not make two. So I gave it to her and said, "Keep this card and don't show it to anybody. It's your Life Card." She assumed that I also had one, even though I didn't.

There were bricks and stones on the side, rubble from bombing during the siege. I thought maybe I would hide under the rubble. Eli said they will search under the rubble and he said, "You stay with us."

So we spent the night like this. The next morning there was a big commotion with everybody running here and there. Eli gave me a piece of paper that was the same size as the Life Card, and he said, "Use this." It was a blank piece of paper.

I had some water and tomatoes, and we ate them. At the same time we could see that all the people of Number Thirteen were very happy, making themselves sandwiches with sardines, the most expensive food. They were eating, laughing, having a good time. Szymek, Lolek, and Eli all said, "These Number Thirteens are finished. We'll see what happens now." They had a suspicion about them. It was on account of the Number Thirteens that many people disappeared. People said, "You will see how they will be laughing in a very short time."

Right away we found out that there would only be two thousand of us that would come back to the brushmaking factory. The rest would go on to the train. Only two thousand.

They marched our factory out. I had a piece of paper. On the paper was nothing, a piece of blank paper. When they said, "March!" I went behind Eli with his mother, his girlfriend, and the child. Szymek with his mother and Lolek were up front. "Ein, zwei, drei—one, two, three!" we went marching, marching. As soon as we marched out of the Umschlagplatz, those happy ones, the Number Thirteens, were not so happy. All of a sudden an SS man shouted, "Halt!" and he pushed us to the front, and pushed the others to the back—the Number Thirteens—to load them onto the trains. Then we marched through the empty streets back to the brushmakers'. I still did not have a Life Card, just the piece of paper with nothing on it. I marched the way we were supposed to march.

When we came back to the brushmakers', there was a table with a green cloth, and at the table there was a German doctor sitting with the Jew who was the director—not the engineer, the big fatso—but another Jew. They were checking the papers.

Naturally, I made sure that my mother went first. She had her card. They did not know her name was not Sofia Goldberg. They passed her. She was happy. Then I stood before them. They asked me for my card. I told the Jew that I did not have my card.

"No!" he said. "You go back!" and he was laughing. "You go back!"

There was already a group of people standing to be sent back to the *Umschlagplatz* so I went and stood with them. I started to cry. This was the first time I broke down. I had never cried in front of them, really. I cried under the pushcart where I slept, but otherwise I did not cry. Yet I started to cry then. So the German doctor looked and said, "Call this *Juden.*" They called me back. He asked the Jew why I was being sent back.

"Because she has no papers."

"So what. She's young. She can work."

"No, no," the Jew said. "My family has been selected, they are at the *Umschlagplatz.* I will exchange her for my family."

"Oh, no," the German said. "You don't exchange her for your family. Your family stays there, and she goes to work!"

Can you understand such things? I don't blame the Jew for wanting to save his family, but it was the German doctor who saved me. So far I had been saved three times by Germans—when I went out from the line with a lot of *chutzpa* to save my mother from selection, when the German soldier gave me a Life Card, and this time when I cried and the German doctor pulled me out of the line for death. I had been saved by some Jews, also. The Jewish policeman who took me off the cart: that was one. Once, another Jewish policeman helped me get away from the SS when there was a roundup at our house.

And so I went back to the brushmakers' factory to work. I was lucky.

But I was still thinking hard about how to escape from the ghetto. I said to my mother, "We are now two thousand in this group. How do we know if tomorrow they won't take the rest? I don't like this. We are coming to the end. There were so many in this factory compound, and now it is quiet, nobody is here."

ESCAPE FROM THE GHETTO

Then who did I meet again on the street but my cousin Janek Mikicinski, the communist Jewish policeman. "You still here?" he asked. "I'll tell you something, give you an idea. You want to get out?"

I said, "Yes."

"Do you have money?"

"I have."

"It costs fifteen hundred *zlotys*. There are smugglers coming into the ghetto with food. They will take you through the sewers. You have to trust them. I don't guarantee anything. They can take away the money if they don't like you, and they can drop you right in the sewers to die. They can take you to the Gentile section and give you away. They can do anything. Or they can take the money and do nothing. You have to take a chance. Do you want to take a chance?"

"Sure I do. And I want to go with this girl, Franka. She knows a Gentile fellow with an apartment and we can stay there until the end of the war," I told him. Franka said she knew this fellow named Janusz, but she didn't have any money. So I told her I would pay for her if she would take me and my mother to this apartment outside of the ghetto. So, Janek told me where to meet the smugglers.

When Helena Goldberg, my friend from Café Sztuka, was taken to the train she left behind winter clothing. She had a warm coat. I took her coat, her clothing, her hat, everything. I took jewelry. I prepared myself for going out the next morning. The smugglers were supposed to come. They were supposed to open the manhole cover. I was so excited that I left all the Star of David arm bands on every blouse and dress. You didn't go in the Aryan section with the stars. But I was so accustomed to wearing them that I got dressed and left them on.

That night I opened the window. We were near the ghetto wall. I opened the window, but we were not supposed to have any lights on. For a moment I forgot and I left the light on, and I said to myself, "God, soon I will be over there. I will reach freedom soon, tomorrow morning." I was so excited, imagining my escape, when, all of a sudden, an SS man on a guard tower on the ghetto wall started shooting at me. He almost killed me.

After this I instructed my mother that she should not move anywhere until I had arranged things. "One thing," I said to her, "Don't trust anybody. Don't tell anybody. Don't tell where I went or how. But when you get a letter from me that you can go, you pay these people and you come, too."

I spent the rest of the night preparing things, cleaning clothing so I should look decent because in the Aryan section there were no Jews running around like rats. There they were living a more normal life than we were. I had a bottle of vodka to give myself courage, and I drank to get drunk.

Suddenly, in the evening, somebody knocked. My mother opened the doors and in came the Jewish police. After certain hours they were not supposed to come. But when she opened the door they entered by force. Someone must have told them I was planning to escape. They came and they brought vodka also.

"Why are you drinking alone?" they asked.

"Because I love it," I said. I was never so drunk that I lost my mind. I could still say what I wanted to say.

"If you have some money, we can help you get out to the Aryan section."

"That's marvelous," I said. "I don't have money now, but I can get it tomorrow. How will you take me out?"

"Through the cemetery."

"That's marvelous," I said.

"Let's make an appointment."

"I'll prepare everything. Tomorrow morning before the break of day, I will be there."

"And you wait for us," they said.

"But will you wait?"

"Sure," they said. "You'll bring the money?"

My mother was ready to tell them I already had the money. "No," she said, "she's got—" I stepped on her foot. I almost killed her.

"How much money? I'll get it."

"What's she saying?" the policeman asked.

"Oh, she doesn't know what she's talking about. You know, mothers don't know what they're talking about."

Finally they left me, figuring I would be there. I wanted to get rid of them.

Morning came. I took a few more good drinks and went down to the street to meet Franka. We were near the wall. Beside the wall there was an entrance where an SS man was marching. Back and forth, marching. Close by was the opening of the sewers.

The smugglers opened the sewers and came one by one. These Gentile fellows were scared, too. They took out a big bottle of vodka and said, "Drink."

"Yes, naturally," I said, and I took a big swig of this vodka. Then they gave it to Franka. She refused. They did not like that at all. She was not a companion, not a comrade. They decided, Zosia takes vodka, she is courageous, she goes first.

We waited as the German marched in our direction. One. Two. Three. Then, when he turned his back, I went into the hole. At first I was going down, and it was all darkness. I didn't exactly fall in, but I tripped down the steps in the wrong way. Slowly, one by one, everybody came. Somebody else who was outside in the ghetto covered the hole so the Germans would not know. The SS man was there, just a few steps from us, but he never saw or heard anything.

When I had prepared myself the night before I took whatever jewelry, gold, and diamonds I could find, along with the money I still had, and I sewed it all into a kind of girdle in such a way that it would be very difficult to find. I also had some extra money in my pocketbook in case they wanted more from me. I paid them right before going down. But I wanted to be able to give them more in case they threatened to abandon us.

One leader, Comrade Ryszard, said to me, "What's your name?"

I told him. He said there would be many places where we would have to swim. "Do you know how to swim?"

I said, "No."

"Give me your pocketbook."

I gave it to him without showing any fear. He liked that, and he put it around his neck with no idea of stealing. He said the same thing to Franka, but she refused. She did everything wrong. So they hated her from the start. When we went through the dirty water of the sewer, through this black, smelly water, they would help her—but only a little bit so she would not drown. Me they held, two men, one by my hands and the other by my legs, as they took me through the waters.

We walked for hours. At one point they got lost and came back to the same spot again. Finally, they found a way and got to the right spot in the Aryan section. Somebody was supposed to open the hole there and let us out. But nobody came. They had a sign. They whistled. Nobody answered. We waited a long, long time, and we were dying of fear. Finally, they all started to pray to Mary. If somebody did not lift the manhole cover, they could not get out and they would have to stay there forever. Finally, somebody came and opened it and we climbed out.

When we got on the tramway, we were so smelly, so dirty, the conductor took one look then looked away. He started to drive the tramway fast, as fast as he could. He started to sing songs like he was coming back from work. It was early in the morning and there was nobody yet on the streets. The smugglers got an idea to sing an insulting song about a Jewess who was selling eggs. I was getting a heart palpitation from fear that this Jewish song would give us away. The smugglers were singing too much about the Jews, and this conductor knew who these two girls were. He saw how we looked.

One thing was certain about the tramways. All the conductors were socialists from Pilsudski's party. They helped the Jews. They helped anybody. They were very good in this way. They were not the so-called intelligentsia. The intelligentsia, Jewish or non-Jewish, they were lousy, the worst. And I don't mean rich ones, but professionals, people with status, education, they were not good. But these conductors were very helpful.

Finally, we got to the Old Town of Warsaw, the part from the times of the kings. The houses were very narrow, very small. They took us to a basement somewhere. They got undressed in front of us and washed themselves with hot water. They were talking and drinking. They asked us what we were going to do. "You have to get out of here very fast. You cannot stay. Only a few hours to rest, then you have to go." Their job was finished.

Then the smugglers started to bet. I had dark hair, dark eyes, and Franka was bleached blond with blue eyes. She did not have bad looks. "You know, we saved them, but which of them will survive the war?"

"Talk to us," they said to me.

"What should I say?"

"Anything. Just talk."

So I talked to them about something. Then they said to Franka, "Now you talk."

When she started to talk, and her Polish sounded more Yiddish than Polish, they said, "Oh, my God, this is some Jewess! She won't survive. She will die. There is no question about this one." Then we straightened ourselves out a little bit and went to the house of this fellow, Janusz, Franka's friend.

I arranged to get my mother. I paid again, and the same smugglers went back and took her out. I don't know what happened to the Jewish police who had visited that night. Maybe they waited for me in the cemetery. Maybe they had some action and they forgot about me. Whatever it was, we were lucky. If they had returned, my mother would never have survived. They would have paid her for what I did because I cheated them. I lied. Anyhow, they did not intend to help me get out. They just intended to get money and give me away.

IN THE ARYAN SECTION

Everything Franka had said was a lie. I thought that Janusz was a friend of her family, but he was her sweetheart. She had told me some story and I believed her. I was also stupid enough to tell her I had jewelry. I had not told her how much, but I had said enough for her to know she could squeeze money out of me.

Meantime, Janusz found us a place to live in the apartment of a widow, a lawyer's wife. She brought in friends of hers, a Jewish woman with children. This woman, along with another woman with small children, all lived on the other side of a partition in the apartment.

One night, I overheard the widow tell the Jewish woman that she and her children were in danger, that the police were coming, and that they should go away. But she did not tell us. She was a good friend to this Jewish woman but not to us. For us it was business only. She did not intend to help us, only to house us. We had no place to go.

So the police came, a plainclothes *Volksdeutscher*. The real Polish police would never come. The Germans would not trust them because the real Polish police would do anything possible against the Germans. He said, "All right, come out!"

I was there in the room, but my mother ran behind a sheet that was hanging in front of some clothing. He said, "I know you're there. Get out!"

All of a sudden I realized this was the end, they had caught us. There was nothing left to do. "Mother, get out from there," I said. "Now you're in the hands of a *Volksdeutscher.*" So he looked at me as if I had insulted him. My mother pinched me, and this time my mother became quite a lady with a lot of brains. She started to cry, to kiss his hands, begging him. "You must help us. I will give you a diamond."

"Let's see this diamond," he said. He could have taken the diamond and finished us off just the same. By then she was saying, "Maybe you knew my husband?" The *Volksdeutscher* police were Germans, but you could still talk to them. Maybe he had even worked for my father.

"Yes, I knew him," he said. "That was your husband? I'll tell you something. He was not my friend because he was too much of a good Pole, but he was a fine man. I'll help you."

He took the diamond and said, "You cannot stay here anymore. I'll just say that you ran away and were not here when I came." And he let us go.

So we were out walking the streets again and we were in real trouble. One day we were walking in a section of Warsaw called Praga. We came across a little house and my mother simply knocked on the door. It turned out that the owner was a tramway conductor. We said we had no relatives and needed a room. "Could you rent us a room?" He looked at us. He understood the situation immediately because no ordinary Pole would come to somebody's house asking for a room. It had to be somebody who had run away from the ghetto. He said, "All right."

"You stay in this room," he said. "You cannot go out. You give me money and I'll buy you food." He was a wonderful person. There was no bathroom, we had to use a pot, so you could imagine the pleasure he had cleaning for us. He had this one room he gave us. He lived in the kitchen with his wife where they would make vodka from cooking alcohol or distilled wood poison.

He was so nice, but he was afraid of his wife. It was my tragedy and misery that I was a very beautiful girl, and he happened to like me. This was my bad luck. He was very respectful and never did anything. But I could feel the way he was looking at me. And his wife noticed how he looked at me, too. She became jealous. While he never did anything wrong, she decided she would turn us in.

One day when she went out to buy food he said, "I cannot keep you anymore because my wife will call the Germans. She told me. Her brother is a very big denouncer who's looking for Jews right and left. They are working with the Germans. I'm afraid of my wife and don't dare say a word because she can say something about me and they'll send me to a camp. So I cannot help you anymore. I'm very sorry. You have to look for some other place. May God help you."

We went out looking, knocking on doors. We found a place with a family, Ukrainians living in Warsaw, extremely pro-German. My mother told them we were from another town and we had had to leave. The woman gave us the apartment. I slept with my mother in the same bed.

But this Ukrainian woman—I can't remember her name—started to get suspicious. She was an anti-Semite who was, as I later found out, actually hunting Jews. In the beginning she helped them, but then once she had gathered enough proof, she gave them away. That was her job—collaborating with the Germans, working for the army.

There was an old house that had been taken over by the German army doctors as a laboratory to check the food the Polish peasants were giving to the army to see that it was not poisoned. She told me, because she suspected we were Jewish, that she would bring me to work in the kitchen of this laboratory. They would give me a card and I could walk in the streets like a human being.

One day this woman took my mother to church. My mother knew nothing of what was going on in the church, so the woman could see something was wrong. She started to press her, and my mother stupidly told her the truth, that we were from the Warsaw Ghetto. "Please keep us. We'll give you money." She was trying to play on the woman's feelings, to get her heart to work. The woman told her not to worry, that she was with good friends.

In the meantime, I worked in the kitchen of the laboratory. There was a maid, a peasant woman, who cooked for the Germans, and I was supposed to peel potatoes for her. The Ukrainian woman arranged for me to live with a Polish teacher in the old part of town and the Germans made me a card so that for the first time, I had papers that were made by the army.

At night, I lived with this teacher, sleeping in the same bed. Her apartment was very close to the ghetto, just on the other side of the walls, and I could hear shooting in the ghetto all the time. I could never sleep at night. I was so edgy. I wanted to cry, and I actually did cry, but in a way that she could not hear. When she heard me, she'd ask why I was crying and I would say I'd had some dream. But the worst part was that this woman, such a nice woman with white hair who looked so beautiful and soft, would say, "Thank God, finally they are killing the Jews. We will get rid of them. There will be no more Jews." She was so happy while I was crying.

THE LABORATORY

I worked in the kitchen of the laboratory feeding the doctors. One of these doctors was always screaming and hollering *"Heil Hitler!"* right and left. But I noticed that whenever some poor man or woman knocked on the door, he would take sausages, butter, chocolate from France, whatever he could get, and would give it to these poor people. And he would give whatever money he had in his pocket. Then he would scream, "Don't you ever knock on this door again!" This German, Dr. Julius Klein, understood Polish but he could not speak it. He was a Catholic from the town of Allenstein in East Prussia near Danzig. I found out later that he was very much against Hitler and the Nazis, but he was pretending because he was afraid of arrest.

This German took a big fancy to me. One day he came into the kitchen. "Show me your hands," he said. I could not speak German, but I understood. He took my hand and said, "You are not a worker. You were never a worker in your life. Wait a second. Wash your hands." He brought me some disinfectant to wash my hands because he was a maniac about bacteria. Then he took me to the laboratory.

He showed me a microscope. "What's that?"

"Microscope," I said in Polish.

"Ah, you know what it is. Good. So you are educated, too. Good, fine. You will be my assistant, my helper. I will teach you laboratory work."

Not only did he teach me laboratory work, he taught me German. Every day he took at least an hour with a pencil, repeating words in German to me. He was teaching me to such an extent that, while I could not speak, I could understand more and more. Eventually, I started to speak a kind of broken German.

He called me by the false name I used for my papers, Irena (or Irene, in German) Olszewska. He was just crazy about me. He was a married man in Allenstein. For Christmas he got a furlough and he went to visit his family, but he immediately came back without completing his vacation to give me the cakes and food that his wife cooked for him. That's how crazy he was. He would say, "When the war is over, I will make a doctor out of you. You will study and go to the university in Warsaw and I will not go back to Germany. This will be Germany anyhow. I'll live in Warsaw and we'll get married." But no matter how good he was, I had nothing really to do with him. This way I was fine. I was correct. It was platonic and he was dreaming.

My mother had been staying with the Ukrainian woman, but suddenly she had no place for her anymore, and my mother was sleeping on the stairs. I wanted to bring her in to stay with me, with the teacher, so under the pretext of Christmas, I asked if I could invite a friend of mine.

Since I had been to Catholic school, I knew everything about Christmas. For me it was easy. Before we left the ghetto I taught my mother catechism and to wear a cross. Some Jews were laughing at us for wearing crosses. They did not know I was preparing myself to be out living amongst Christians.

So my mother came to stay for a Christmas party at the teacher's place. I had all this delicious food that Dr. Klein had brought me from Allenstein. My mother was having difficulty, and when the teacher heard my mother, she said, "I don't know. She must be a Protestant. There's something wrong with her, she's talking nonsense."

Instead of keeping quiet, my mother went to help with Christmas dinner. She was spoiling everything with her talk. The woman got angry with her and said she couldn't stay overnight, and my mother left. I cried because I was able to stay while she was stranded outside in the freezing weather.

For Christmas the doctors invited the Gestapo to a big party. There were some high officers, all these doctors, women Gestapo, and German women who worked with the electricity and telephone companies. Dr. Klein invited me to come. The party was supposed to end very late, after the curfew, so he said he could take me home on the tramway. Poles could go out after the curfew only if they were with a German.

"You have to help in the kitchen," the doctor had said earlier, so I helped make salads and prepare dishes. The cook was furious. She and the others knew I was Jewish. The Ukrainian woman had told them, after my mother confessed to her that we had escaped from the ghetto. The cook was terribly jealous that they took me from the kitchen, from peeling potatoes, to work in the laboratory.

At the head of the dining room was the General, a doctor, and behind him a big picture of Hitler on the wall. I sat next to Julius Klein as his assistant. They served us drinks. They gave me plenty and I drank. I could usually get drunk and still remember what I should or shouldn't say. But sometimes I could slip and say things I was not supposed to.

By this time, I had gotten myself nicely drunk. While they were serving, I noticed that one of the Gestapo men would not stop looking at me. At that time I had long, bleached blond hair, the lightest blond possible, and I had plucked my eyebrows so as not to look so dark. But he was watching me suspiciously. He asked Klein who I was, how I came to work there, and so forth. Then he asked me directly, so I pretended I did not understand him.

I was already drunk, and that Hitler on the wall bothered me a lot. So I got some bravura, and I said in Polish things like, "Why doesn't he drop dead!" But this Gestapo man understood. So Julius Klein got panicky, scared. He pinched me and sent me roughly to the kitchen to fetch something. He went after me. "Keep quiet! Shut up! What are you talking about? Bring this out and don't say a word."

When I came back, they were singing songs. Someone asked me, "Do you know some songs?"

"Yes, I know some," I said. So I sang the Polish national anthem. When they heard that, they just looked at each other. I spoke a lot of nonsense.

The next morning Julius Klein told me that the next time I spoke like this, I would go to jail and he would not be able to help me. "I know how you feel, but you cannot say these things in front of the Gestapo!"

The following day, the Ukrainian woman came to get food from the doctors, and she started to cough. Dr. Klein examined her and immediately took a sample of her phlegm and looked at it under a microscope. "You have tuberculosis, and you didn't tell me. You could infect us!"

The Ukrainian woman looked at me. I had not known she had it. I thought she had a bad cold. Besides, even if I had known she had tuberculosis, even if she had told me to sleep with her in the same bed, I would have slept with her. Nobody thought about health, only about survival. And why would I reveal her secret when she helped me, gave me work, food, and a place to sleep? But she decided that this was the time to denounce me because she might lose her position with the Germans.

I felt a funny atmosphere at work. A few women in uniform came for a visit. They were talking with Klein in low, German voices. I already understood. They were saying, "Poor girl. She is probably from the ghetto, that's what it is. When she was singing so much, she couldn't hide her feelings because she was drunk. She must be Jewish." And Julius Klein said, "I don't think so. Maybe, but I don't think so."

He took me home without saying anything. I started to wonder. I did not know that I had already been denounced, but I started to get very frightened. That night I was thinking whether I should go back to work or just never show up. Maybe I should go out into the streets with my mother again. But I decided to wait and find out. Maybe they were just suspicious.

When I came to work the next morning, Julius Klein called me to his office in the laboratory.

"Who are you?" he asked.

"You know who I am. I am Polish."

"No!" he screamed at me. "Who are you?"

"I am Polish." So he called the cook.

"Juda," she said. She could not speak German. She only knew one word, and she repeated it a hundred times. *"Juda! Juda! Juda!"*

"Are you Jewish?" he asked me.

"No," I answered, very calmly.

There was a man who was cleaning the floors. He called him over. "Who is she?" he asked him. And the man looked at me.

"What are you asking? She is just like me, Polish." He had actually known from the beginning. I knew by the looks he gave me. He would smile and give me winks, not to flirt with me but to let me know we were friends. "She is not Jewish," he said. "Who said so? She is Polish."

I knew that Julius Klein was a good man, that he screamed a lot of *"Heil Hitler!"* at the same time he helped people with money and food and medicine. But I did not know to what extent I could count on him. He threw out this man and the cook, yelling, "Get out! Get out with your dirt! Get out! You don't know anything. You are liars! You are all liars!"

He was hollering on purpose. When the doors closed he took a gun and he put it to my forehead and he said, quietly, "Who are you? And you better tell me the truth. Now nobody hears but me."

What should I do? I knew one thing about good Germans. If you told them a lie they would hate you like poison. But you could never tell a bad German the truth. I said to myself that I would take a chance.

"Yes, I am Jewish."

He put away his gun and started to cry. "Oh, my God. Oh, my God. What have I done? You, my beloved girl, you are Jewish? This is terrible. They will send me to the Russian front. I don't know what I will do now."

In Poland, the German laws were such that if somebody said you were a Jew there were no questions asked. They did not even bother beating you. They would take out a gun and kill you on the spot. No German man could have any kind of contact with a Jewish woman, especially not sexual relations. If he did, he would be demoted and sent to Russia immediately. They were all scared of going to the Russian front because the Germans there were suffering from the terrible cold. They were freezing without proper clothing. They were not prepared. They were wearing galoshes in the snow and they were losing legs in the frost. They laughed at the Russians who wore rugs and paper on their feet, but that was the thing to wear. So Klein was very afraid of being sent to the Russian front.

He put his finger to his mouth, signaling me to be quiet and he showed me to the door while he repeated, "These Poles, they are liars!" He wanted to get me out of the office onto the street to protect me because, now that I had been denounced, the Gestapo would come and kill me. He screamed, pretending he did not know, so that he would not be guilty of his connection with me. But he also wanted to get me out of there, as if he did not really believe I was Jewish. He took me out on the street and said, "My God, you are a poor girl. Where is your mother?"

"My mother is here somewhere."

"And where is the rest of the family?"

"They have been killed."

He began to carry on. "Look, you can never come back to this job. Change the place where you live. Don't go to sleep there anymore. They will go after you because I will say I was the stupid one that let you get away but I did not know. I did not believe you were Jewish. But you must get away because they will kill you. Take this for when you need something, when you are in trouble ..." He tried to give me money, but I did not accept it. "If you need money, or are hungry, just call me up on a telephone. You call me, and then I will meet you somewhere. But do not ever come back here anymore."

I really hope that he was not sent to the Russian front. After the war was over, I sent letters to Allenstein in his name. The letters did not come back, but I never found out if he was dead or alive. If he is alive, he should live long and be very healthy, because he saved my life.

ON THE STREET

From then on I was on the street with my mother, sleeping in stairways. It was the winter of 1942, an awful winter with tremendous snow. We were too afraid to go to the store where we could buy hot soup, so we just kept on marching. It was not for lack of money that we did not go to the store but because we did not look, so to say, kosher. We looked like bums on the streets. One day I found a piece of bread on the snow. I picked it up and we ate it together. We were starving and dirty. And the worst part is that we were covered with lice.

We got a sickness from the dirt and lice, mange itch in English. We thought we would die from this rash over our entire bodies. I was scratching myself so much that I was bleeding. So one day I saw a name, M.D., on a house. I said I would go to the doctor. "I can't stand it anymore. I need medicine."

I went to this doctor. I told him I had a rash, although I already knew what it was. I got undressed and he looked at this bitten body.

"Oh, this is from dirt," he said. "How is a young girl like you so dirty? How is it possible?" And then he started to look suspicious while he asked questions. He was not a dumbbell. "Ah," he said. "Ah, I understand. Wait a second."

I got scared. I thought he was calling up the police to denounce me. But he went to the other room and got a bottle of medicine which he gave to me, and he said, "There are many Turkish baths. Just go there early in the morning. First cover yourself with the medicine and then bathe. And then again cover yourself with the medicine and again wash." It was very dangerous to go. But we did it.

We had the most awful times on the streets. When night came and we wanted to sleep out of the snow, we climbed up the stairs to the attic of a house without anybody seeing us. Both of us slept inside a baby carriage. I will never forget that carriage with the rats crawling in. Then in the morning we were afraid to go out because the building super might see us and call the police, immediately thinking that we were thieves. Oh, that was some suffering, going from house to house, walking, just walking and walking.

My mother wanted to make her hair blond, so she dyed her hair. But it became red, so red that it looked like those clowns with painted red hair. She looked like a hundred Jewesses because of this red hair. Many Jews in Warsaw were redheaded, like the Irish. She looked so bad she wore a *babuszka,* a big kerchief, to cover her face. She looked old, like sixty, although she was not that age at all. At least no one would look at her. She was old, yet we looked alike, which was very dangerous.

I was almost exposed three times when I was on the street. Several times I saw the trucks with the *placowka,* the Jews who worked outside the ghetto, and many times they would holler, "Zosia, how are you?!" I made believe I didn't know them when they yelled from the trucks because if some Gentile would see that, they would know right away that I was Jewish. They were not doing it on purpose to give me away, they were just hollering hello, happy to see someone they knew.

Another time there was one fellow by the name of Lifszitz whom I had known from before the war. He was tall and skinny, with curly, kinky, blond hair, and he worked for the Germans. I was told that he would go into the Aryan section and he would look for Jews to denounce. One day I saw Lifszitz on the street, and he was heading in my direction. So I went up to him, right up to him, and I said, "You know, I have a knife. I will stab you if you try to give me away. Get away!" He ran away from me; otherwise I would have been in big trouble.

Then one day I met my old history teacher, Mrs. Dinces, who was also the wife of the director of my *gymnasium.* Mr. Dinces had changed his faith and become a Catholic, but that wouldn't keep his wife safe. She spoke Polish, not Yiddish, and her Polish was so beautiful it was like music, yet now she was running away with her daughter. She had blond hair with very thick braids in the back. When she saw me I almost went over to her to say hello, but she got so scared that she crossed the street and ran away from me. I don't blame her—she was afraid of me, she didn't know who I was. These were the three times that I met people, and each time I could have been exposed or denounced.

Once, my mother tried to look up some friend of my father, someone whom my father had saved from the Russians when he and the others tried to drive off with the Polish treasury. He used to have a villa not far from us in a small town near Warsaw. So she went there to see if he could help us, maybe give us a place to live or sleep. She came to him and he recognized her despite the way she looked. She told him that her husband was already dead, that she had run away with her daughter, and could they help her. "Get out!" he said. "I don't keep Jews. I would have helped your husband because he was my friend. He was not a Jew." My father looked 100 percent Gentile. This man knew my father was a Jew, but to him he was not. So that was one more place we could not go, and we continued walking the streets.

Everybody had to have a *Ken Karte,* a registration card with a photo showing the left ear along with three quarters of the face, showing the nose and cheeks. The Nazis said an ear could be a Jewish ear. If your nose stuck out too much, you were Jewish. If your eyes stuck out, you were Jewish. These were their racial ideas, so we had to have this ID card.

I did not have it, but I did have a card from the Germans from when I was working in Dr. Klein's laboratory. It was such a good card I did not throw it away.

One day I was walking with my mother when I heard somebody behind us. I could tell we were about to be picked up, so I said to her, "Let's go fast."

"What?" she asked, "What are you doing?"

"Go fast," I said. "Get away from me! Get away!"

Anyone could stop you; they did not have to be the police. Many people made believe they were police. They were simply denouncers trying to scare people to get money. They were completely without heart. And there was no way to get away from them. Once you were in their hands, and once you showed them you were scared, you were finished. You could never admit to them that you were Jewish. In Poland, when someone said, "I am sure she is Jewish, no question about it," you were gone, shot. Then they took you away and threw you on the garbage. In Germany they had to beat you, torture you, and ask questions until you confessed. They were still obeying some kind of international law. As long as your offense was not proven, they could not kill you. In Germany they took more care. In Poland they shot you down.

The man who was following us tapped me on the shoulder. "You are two Jewesses," he said.

I had learned how to respond from a Gentile friend of my father. Back when we were in the ghetto he had come to tell us that the Jews were being killed and we should get out. He said to me, "Remember one thing. You are not Jewish. They cannot pull down your pants and check if you are a Jew. When somebody attacks you, never show fear. Use vulgar words like anybody else, the most dirty words so that you sound sure of yourself. And attack *them!*"

So that's what I did. I started to curse, saying, "You are insulting me. *You* are a Jew." We had a big fight. I didn't know if this man was a policeman or just somebody looking for Jews to get money. He was probably most interested in first getting money from Jews, then he would always have time to give them away, maybe even find more Jews, a whole family or others who might have been hiding.

He pulled us over to the doorway of a building. "Don't scream so much. Don't make such a noise. Come on, come on. Show me your papers."

"Who are you," I said, "that I should show you papers? Show me *your* papers!" He showed me something very fast and I knew that he was not the police. Then I asked him if he knew different people with the police. These were real people, but I knew they were not with the police anymore. This was just to show I knew some important people in the police.

"All right," I said, "You want to see? Here it is." And I showed him the German card from the laboratory that said I was working for the army and gave my name and address. He looked at it, then he looked at my face and it looked good to him.

All the while I was talking to him, I was stepping on my mother's foot, hinting to her to get away. He was so busy with me that he had forgotten her completely. But she did nothing. My mother, how could she leave her baby? She would not let go of me, although I was pinching her and pushing her. I was surprised he did not see that. She was lucky because he did not even look at her. There was nothing interesting about her. He gave me back my card.

"What money do you have?" he asked.

"What money?" I exclaimed. "You are very lucky that I don't go to the police to say that you bother people. Just get away and that's all! Goodbye!" I took my mother and left him.

"First we walk," I told my mother. I looked sideways to see if he was coming after us. First he was thinking, not knowing if he had done well or not in letting us get away. Then I saw a tramway station. Ho, ho, my friends the tramway conductors! So I told my mother, "Now we run!"

We jumped on the tramway though we did not have the money to pay. This conductor did not even know what had happened, he just started to fly down the tracks. The man was running around one side of the tramway to the other. But we had gotten down on the floor where other people were sitting so he could not see us. The other passengers did not do anything. They could see that something was happening, but they got scared. He did not know which direction we were heading, so he gave up and ran off.

We got off the tramway far away, who knew where? It did not matter to us since we had no place to sleep anyhow. Any house was as good as another, so we climbed into another attic. "You give me your clothing," I told my mother, "and I'll give you mine." Then we separated, going in different directions, after arranging to meet at a particular place.

Afterward, I met the man who was a friend of my father, the same one who had given me the idea that no matter how they beat you, never confess. He was an engineer named Jerzy. We went to a tearoom to sit down. He ordered tea for me, but he would not sit next to me. He was afraid to sit with me, and he sat like he did not know me. I was at one table and he was at another. In case they caught me, he had nothing to do with me.

"I am very sorry I cannot take you to my house," he said. "But my wife looks like a hundred Jewesses. All the time I have trouble with the police. From time to time I have to go to the police to present her and show her papers to prove she is not Jewish. So it is out of the question for you to come. And your mother better not come either." He did not like my mother. In his eyes my mother was too Jewish, so she should never come to him because he would denounce her. He told me that. All his goodness of heart was for me only.

"Go on this street," he said. "Go until you see people getting arrested. They are rounding up the youth to send to Germany to work—forced labor. You will be forced to work on a farm or in a factory. If you are not bombed and if nobody denounces you, you will survive the war this way. Here you have no chance. Separate from your mother because she's worse for herself and for you. You have to separate. You cannot go on together."

So that's what I decided to do.

"STUPID GIRL, YOU ARE GOING TO GERMANY!"

I was walking one day and got myself caught with a group of other Polish youth. I did not have papers, but many Polish youngsters did not have papers. They would leave the house to go to the store to get cigarettes or buy something, if only for a moment, and they would be caught. Many times the Germans would catch them when they went for a bottle of beer. Right outside their house. Or if they slept overnight at a friend's house. Or if they forgot their papers. Or if they did not have them or if they had false papers like me.

They sent us to a detention camp that was located in some kind of public school, a big building where they kept all Polish youths in different rooms according to which towns they came from, to be sent out to Germany as soon as possible. They put me in a room for all those caught from the town of Zyrardow.

We slept in bunks, one on top of the other. I took a higher bunk to be away from people because I was afraid of sicknesses, infections. There were a lot of things going around. But I took that bunk also to be far away from anyone who might recognize me. That would have been a problem.

On the lowest bunk was a beautiful blond girl with a beautiful figure. I saw her nude when we were examined. She was gorgeous, maybe fifteen or sixteen. One day, she was lying on her bunk and some boys and girls came around and said, "You stole our songs." They were looking for a book of songs.

"No," she said, "I didn't take it." When they heard her Jewish accent, they took her by the hair and beat her up good and gave her away to the Germans. She was killed. And I was in the bunk next to her.

When I stood nude for my medical examination, a German soldier, when he saw me, almost vomited. I still had pimples, this itchy disease. Nearly everybody had the same disease. I was not alone. Everybody was suffering from this itch. I had found my element in which to hide. All the Poles had the same thing. They were also living in the ruins. Who knew how they were caught, and in what condition? They were runaways. They were in the underground. They had beat up some German, killed some German. There were all kinds of stories attached to these young people.

A German doctor saw me. "What is that?" he asked. "Syphilis?"

I only knew how to say, *"Kratzen, Kratzen."*

"Ah, *Kratzen." Kratzen* means "scratch," "itch." He was only afraid this was syphilis. I was covered all over. Pimples everywhere. It surprised me I did not have them on my face. For years I had those marks on my body. Whatever was scratched became a scar.

The doctor gave me the same medicine he gave everyone else, a smelly gray paste. We washed. Then the paste. Then we washed again. The first time I got rid of it, I was so grateful that they had cleansed me of that disease. You have no idea how good I felt.

They called every morning, "Who wants to go to work?" I was ready for anything. I was already peeling potatoes, washing floors, anything just to be busy and to show I was willing to work. One day they asked, "Who can type? Who wants to work in the office?" Then all of a sudden I heard my name—the false name I had given, Olszewska. They must have been looking for this woman because she was Jewish.

I felt sick to my stomach when I heard that name. I did not know how or why they came looking for me. While I was working they did not ask me about my name, but when I finished I changed to another room, moving from Zyrardow to some other town. I just changed rooms and began sleeping there.

One woman came over to me. "You know something," she said, "You look very interesting to me. I would like very much to see your hand."

Hitler was once told by a fortune-teller that he would lose the war, that he would die, all the worst things. From then on, whoever told fortunes went to the worst camps, like Buchenwald, Dachau, or Auschwitz. They were finished.

That woman took my hand. She looked at it and said, "You will be beaten. And at one point you are supposed to die. I cannot look at your hand." She threw away my hand and did not want to say anything more. She just ran away from me. When I heard that, I changed rooms again.

They called my name many times, but I never answered. Whenever they called my name, I wasn't there. But I had a big problem. I could not get out from that detention center. New bunches of people kept coming. There were others who had already been staying there pretty long. They wondered why I was still there.

The Polish girls were terribly afraid to go to Germany alone, so fake marriages became common. They would say that they were married to somebody in order to go with a fellow who was supposed to protect them. They figured they would be defended or helped.

So one day some young Polish fellow—he seemed pretty stupid—came to me. This fellow began telling me some kind of story. And then he said, "How about if we get married? We'll get married and we'll go together. I like you."

I looked at him and said to myself, "That's my victim." His name was Marian Wrobleski. I became Mrs. Wrobleska, in the Polish form for a married woman. Now I was married. Naturally, we only said that we were married, and no marriage ever took place. I did not have papers, but he did, and so I got papers. They believed him when he said I was his wife. So when they next called "Wrobleski," he said, "Here I am, but I don't want to go without my wife."

"Good, Wrobleski and Wrobleska, go!" So the police took us to the train. The police were *Volksdeutschers*. Maybe some were Polish, or maybe they worked with the underground. You didn't know what they were doing. But when they were marching close to the train, some of these policemen were saying, "Run away! Run away!" There was a way to run away into a crowd of people. At one point there were parents crying, families standing there. So if you ran fast you could have gotten to these groups of families. One of the policemen pushed me to go to these crowds. I pushed him away. He did not understand that I wanted to go to the train.

"Stupid girl, where are you going? You are going to Germany!"

I did not even answer him. I wanted to go to Germany because there was no other way to hide anymore. The Germans came with their bayonets. "Faster! Faster!" And we got on the train. When the train started we sang the Polish anthem, crying. I was crying like a baby, too. This was the last time I saw Poland.

It was a cold winter day with heavy snow falling on the fields. And we were going, going, on the train to Germany. They gave us bread cut in half with marmalade. The train was all closed off. I think it was a cattle train. The part of the train where the Germans were was warm, and they were sitting there watching us.

I do not know where, near the frontier, maybe already in Germany somewhere, wherever it was, I saw Jews wearing yellow stars working the fields. I took my bread and I threw it out the window. And we all started to throw our bread to the Jews through the windows.

I left my mother in Warsaw. I learned later that she went

back to the room with the Ukrainian woman, and then found another room. She got herself papers. She became smart when I was gone.

One day she saw Lutek Trauman, the son of her aunt Telca, who was also hiding in an apartment in the Aryan section. She told him that Zosia had gotten herself caught by the Germans. "If she is so smart," Lutek said, "I'll be smart, too. I'll do the same thing." He let himself be caught for forced labor.

But Lutek forgot one thing—he was a man. Whenever the Germans would catch the youth, they would check to see if those they caught were healthy, that they did not have syphilis. They would pull down their pants to make an examination. He got himself caught, but when they pulled down Lutek's pants and they saw that he was circumcised, he was killed.

FORCED LABOR

Our train finally reached its destination, although I don't know where we were exactly. Somewhere in the northwest part of Germany. They took us to *Arbeitsfront,* the place where they assigned work. The Germans came and looked at us in the way you hear in stories about Negro slaves in the South. They looked at us to tease. They touched our muscles, looking at our teeth, our eyes.

They looked me over and took me to a job together with Marian Wrobleski because we were married. We went to the farm of an old man named Albrecht. He had two pieces of property, one in the town of Aime and the other in the town of Duingen, where he lived with his wife and children. We went to Aime where there was just a housekeeper and a lot of workers and the old man's daughter, Elizabeth. French prisoners of war were also there helping. During the day they were taken out in the fields by the Germans to work.

I worked mostly in the house and not so much in the fields. Wrobleski was working in the fields. I did not want to be with that fellow, but I was stuck. He had his nails in me. He would beat me, and I would beat him back. Screaming all the time. I did not want any part of him. He was filthy, terrible, nuts. I made believe I married him only because I wanted to get out of the detention camp.

Then he started to wonder why I went with him. "Why did you go with me, if you didn't want me? You must have some reason." He was thinking and thinking. Then he started to get ideas.

"I know you are a Jew," he said. "You are a Jew. You just wanted to use me to get out from there. I know."

Now I was in his hands and his goodness if he wanted
to give me away or not. He beat me and screamed, and the
farmers could not understand the situation. But they somehow saw that I didn't fit that young fellow. These Germans
saw I was so unhappy that they tried to split us up as much
as they could. They took sympathy for me and sometimes at
four o'clock, which was their time to have coffee and cake,
they would scream at me, "Come here, you have to help!"
They pretended that they were giving orders, but they were
really calling me to have coffee and cake and sit at the same
table with them.

Albrecht's daughter, Elizabeth, was teaching me German, and I was teaching her French. It was an exchange of
languages. They even gave me aquatints with which to paint.
They were wonderful to me; they were wonderful people. I
wondered why they were so unbelievably good.

The owner, Albrecht, had young children, but he was
a very old man. He and his wife had a child of eleven or
twelve who was in the *Hitlerjugend,* the Hitler Youth. He was
the most awful little bandit. The whole family was afraid of
him. When he was around they screamed all day, *"Heil
Hitler!"* When he was gone, they would stop. When he was
around they would not invite me for coffee and cake. They
were afraid, afraid of neighbors, afraid of each other. Whenever a neighbor came with something, they always screamed
and talked about the Jews.

But one day Elizabeth was giving me cake and we were
talking—you know, this exchange of languages. I spoke
enough German by that time, not well, but enough to speak
fairly fluently. "Tell me, what happened to the Jews in
Poland?" she asked. I was a little bit surprised when she
asked me. It scared me a little bit.

"Oh, you know," I said, "The Jews are being killed." For
a moment she was silent.

"Well, *la guerre est comme la guerre,"* she said, War is like war, as if she accepted that this was a normal part of the war. We did not have radios and got no news. We did not know how the war was going. We wanted to find out what was happening. We did not know if the Germans were winning. Whenever you saw slogans on the walls, they said they were winning, always winning.

We sent letters to our families in Poland. When we were writing to them, we gave names to the English, the Americans, and the Russians, names like Tony or Peter or Paul. When one of the Allies advanced, it was written like a family fight. So if Paul got beaten up, it meant the Russians had lost a battle. There were a lot of family quarrels. So that's how we knew that the Russians were coming or going, whether the Russians were losing. We had, so to speak, our own news. But that was only hearsay. We could not be sure of anything, we really did not know how the war was going.

So I made contact with the French prisoners of war who helped me start my own underground. They had a radio, and they listened for news constantly. They would tell us what was going on. I met some fellow from Belgium, one of the prisoners. Adolph—his name was Adolph too, ha! I liked him very much, and he liked me, too. He would come and tell me everything.

Then I got sick and I was sent to a military hospital in the little town of Gronau.

"IT'S A LONG WAY TO TIPPERARY"

When I first got to the hospital in Gronau all the French prisoners of war would sneak through the window to bring me goodies—milk and chocolates, everything. In the bed next to me was a woman, a teacher, Teresa Koschmider. She was Polish, from Lodz originally, but she had been living near Warsaw when she was captured for forced labor in Germany. She was the first one to give me news of the burning of the Warsaw Ghetto, of the uprising.

She was in the hospital because she had lost three fingers from her hand. She had been working with some machine that tore off her fingers. It was a simple accident. She hated the Germans. Teresa also got in contact with the French POWs. She was a good Polish patriot and she definitely did not do good work for the Germans. Wherever she was, she was trying to sabotage the Germans rather than help them. She was always talking because others were often ignorant, so she had to clear up their heads on the point of Germany.

She probably knew that I was Jewish without ever asking. She did not ask me because she did not want to scare me. The Polish, when they were nice, they were really nice. They pretended they did not know. They did not ask questions. If they asked, and if the Germans beat them later, they would have to talk, to save themselves from pain. She never asked.

But one day she gave me a Bible and said, "Pray. Here is a letter that I got from Warsaw." And there it was in the letter—they were burning the Jews. They were falling from the windows, there were fires all over, all the most terrible things. "Turn your head to the wall," she told me, as if to tell me to go ahead and cry to myself peacefully.

I developed a very high fever. German soldiers were coming to the hospital from the Russian front. They would have a head but no hands. No arms, no legs—they had frozen and fallen off. They were like cadavers with no ears. Or one arm and no legs. I had never seen anything like it. In my high fever I began to sing songs to myself. Like "It's a long way to Tipperary, it's a long way to go ..." In English. This was a big problem. Here I was a peasant, not supposed to speak any languages, and I was singing in English surrounded by these cadavers, all because I was delirious.

There was another Polish girl in the room, Wladka. She was a real peasant, a stupid little girl. She knew nothing. But there was also a Ukrainian woman in my room. One day out of the blue she went out into the corridor speaking to the nurses, to the doctors. "She's a Jew! She's a Jew!" Not only that, but behind the doors of this hospital a Gestapo man stood, watching. They respected the international law that if you were in a hospital you could not be touched. They did not bother you, but as soon as you left the hospital you would be arrested. So they watched me from behind the doors.

I kept on singing in my fever. I was getting all ready. Even in my fever, I knew they would take me away. There was no way for me to run. That's what I figured at that moment, and that's why I sang like this. It was like a pain in the back, and I relieved it with singing. I could be killed at any moment.

Meanwhile, I had managed to make contact with my mother. She had sent me a letter that had come to the farm, and then I got another letter from the engineer, the friend of my father, who had told me to get caught for forced labor. One day in despair my mother had gone to see him in Warsaw. She could not go on any more, she was so frozen, so exhausted. She asked him to give her a room. He told her to wait and kept her in the kitchen. He went to the telephone and called the Germans, which is exactly what he said he would do if she came again. She smelled something was wrong. She did not know they were coming, but she left. She went down as the Germans arrived and they asked her where this apartment was, about this Jewish woman. She said, "It's over there." She showed them and walked out. It was like God wanted her to be saved.

Both of these letters told me what had happened. They were dangerous to have. I tore these two letters into the smallest pieces. Even the stamps. Fever or no fever, I swallowed them. I was in a very bad condition. I could not swallow. I was not drinking water or milk or anything. But I knew only one thing: despite all this I had to swallow those letters.

One nurse, a nun, would come in the nighttime with injections to help me. She said, "I have to give you something to give you strength, something that will help you a lot." All night she fed me by force even though I did not want to eat. There were no vitamins in those times, but she was giving me something like them to give me strength. She would tell me she was giving me something, but always with her finger up like I should not talk about it. During the day, nothing. Nobody took care of me during the day.

I had one other night nurse. She was not a nun and she would say, "Maybe, when you get better, I'll ask the *Arbeitsfront* if you can work for me. You will take care of my child, and I will take care of you." Both of these nurses were just good people. They were very sorry for me.

One day, the Germans gave me injections to force me to talk. I knew they were putting me to sleep with the injections.

"What's your name?" they asked. "What's your name?"

I only heard myself saying one thing, "Hitler, why don't

you drop dead!" And I did not hear my name. That's all. I don't know what I said later. Only, "Hitler, drop dead!" and I fell asleep.

In the morning, a Czech woman who was collaborating with the Germans came and she said to me, "Who is Goldberg?" I must have said something in my sleep. Because they could not break my mind, they used these injections.

I got such a fear from all these shots that I stopped talking. One day I lost my voice completely. I wanted to say something. Nothing would come out. Wladka ran out and called the nurse. The nurse forced the German doctor to come. It looked like I was dying of a heart attack or something. The doctor examined me and said that I had a heart like a horse, and he pushed me out of fury that I was not dying from a heart attack. The nurse gave me a shot and my voice came back. It was probably from fear that I lost my voice.

The French prisoners of war were still coming and looking after me, telling me not to worry, something will happen, I will survive the war—giving me pep talks. Finally, the fever went down. My clothing had been taken away from me, but I found it. When the nurse left, I went slowly to the bathroom. I got dressed and jumped out of the window. I ran away from the hospital and the Gestapo, even though I was still not well.

I got back to the farm in Duingen. I could go no farther. I was not well. Finally, the farmer sent my "husband" and me to a semi-camp, a factory, because he got scared about keeping me. But he asked us to come to his house in the evening when I was free.

One day I came, and he walked out with me. He made sure nobody was behind the bushes. He was always looking, making sure. "I don't know who you are. And I won't ask you. But cash will help you survive the war," and he gave me some money. "Let me tell you something. You see this farm, all these hills. They are not mine. They belong to Jewish people, although they were taken away a long time ago. There is only the grandmother left. This was her farm."

If you were a German Jew, and you were a woman of ninety or ninety-five, they let you live. They did not take you to camp, because you were dying anyhow and they did not want to bother. But you had to be a real German Jew. So these farmers kept her in some room they had, and they would bring her food.

SABOTAGE

When I arrived at the factory camp to work, they did not know I had run away from the hospital. They were very well organized, but it was war and even the Gestapo had mix-ups. They did not expect me to be there so they did not look for me.

In this factory the Germans were making boxes for bombs. We were resisting, sabotaging without stop. The Russian workers would hit back at the Germans. For that they would be terribly beaten, tortured, and they would go to the camps, maybe not to come back alive. Polish people were more compliant, working more peacefully. They did not want to be beaten, they did not want to go to a camp. But whenever there were some people from Warsaw, there was sabotage. People from Warsaw normally never went to work without doing some sabotage. The Ukrainians, however, were traitors. They were working against the Russians, against the Poles, against everybody, denouncing all the time.

When we were at the farm, I also did sabotage. We were supposed to cut the weeds, to separate them from the vegetables that were growing. But we would cut the weeds in such a way that the roots stayed. So when the first rain came, the roots would get even bigger and damage the crop. Our idea was to make the Germans hungry. If they were not able to eat, the war would finish faster. We could not throw bombs, so we were doing what we could—sabotage, all the time.

But it was never done by talking to each other. Only by look. Never organized, just done. We went in groups of people to work. We only had to look at each other and we knew what it was about. We knew that we were working for the enemy.

I never had contact with resistance organizations. There were very strong organizations in Poland, partisans, but I had no contact. In the ghetto, maybe those who were already in parties would be connected. If people were not with a party, they would not even know. And there was the need for secrecy. To get out from the ghetto I had to be secret. You did not know who you could trust.

There was sabotage even by the Jewish police, who were make-believe police, like my cousin, Janek Mikicinski. He was not a real policeman. He just wore a policeman's hat. He was a fake one in order to get people out from the ghetto for the resistance. Or like my cousin, Janka Lubelska, who was a prison guard. She was passing papers and food, medicine, and all kinds of things through. So plenty of sabotage was done. But you would not know about it.

Resistance outside of the ghetto was more open. The ghetto was in a bad position. In America and in Great Britain there were Jewish organizations that were sending money for arms. But we never got these armaments, the Polish Home Army kept them for themselves. They would not give them to us. It was not correct. The Polish Army would not even give us the chance to die in honor, because we had nothing to fight with. Polish partisans had guns, they had something to fight with, grenades. They were producing bombs. But we had no dynamite. The Jews had nothing.

So there, in Germany, in the factories, I saw resistance everywhere. Sabotage everywhere. I did sabotage myself and I got into trouble for it. Being Jewish, instead of sitting quietly and never moving or talking to anybody, I had to make sabotage.

One day when I went to work, a German engineer who was drawing up plans asked, "Who knows how to draw?" I said, "I do." I always pushed myself to work. He gave me pencils and everything I needed to draw. He was an older German. If they were young, they were 100 percent Nazi and were awful and hated us like poison. The older Germans felt sorry for us, although they could not do much. I worked for this engineer from time to time.

I sent my mother a letter. She knew where I was living, and she would write to me as if I was a friend and she was an old maid named Dimka. She had moved from Warsaw and gone to Krakow. There she had no place to live. She had walked and walked until she found by coincidence a very dear friend of my father. Her name was Fela, and she was married to an officer who was a Polish border guard. She was a great patriot, too, a Jewish woman married to a Gentile. Maybe because she had been in love with my father (I do not know these private matters)—at least she had liked my father very much—she decided to help my mother.

Fela was hiding also. Her husband was missing at the border—maybe he had run away—but she had false papers. She was working for the Germans in a canteen, and the Germans did not know she was Jewish at all. She looked like a Gentile, very blond, pale.

Fela helped my mother to get a place. My mother got a job as a maid taking care of the child of a German family. She stayed with this family through the rest of the war. The man was actually not German but Austrian, and the woman was Czech. The man was not bad to my mother, but the woman was terrible. My mother had many problems with her.

Anyway, my mother decided to send me a package of food through Fela. She bought raisins and cans of sardines. She told Fela I was in Germany. Fela worked in the canteen and knew all the officers, and one of them was going on furlough. Fela gave the package to him to deliver to me because his town was close to me.

All of a sudden, one day, a German soldier came with a package. He spoke to me. "Do you know Fela?" he asked.

I did not know who he was talking about, this Fela. Maybe they were confronting me, the Gestapo. "No, I don't know Fela."

"What do you mean, you don't know her? Why did she send you a package?" He showed me a picture of her. I thought he probably had some affair with her, who knows?

"I don't know that woman," I said. "Maybe I knew her as a child, I don't know." I did not know why he came. He started to ask too many questions and I got scared that he was the Gestapo. So he left the package, but he was very suspicious. He went and checked with the factory office, which did not help me.

I would always keep quiet in my bunk. I was all alone in this place. Since I was Jewish, I was actually much less afraid than any of the Ukrainians, Poles, French, or Germans. If there was sabotage I did it without any fear whatsoever because I knew that to go to prison for sabotage for me was a very small matter. If I were taken for the real stuff, for being a Jew, I would be killed. For me, then, it did not matter if I were taken for sabotage. I was really not afraid. So I hid all kinds of cards and papers, even political documents, in my room. To some extent the other women were taking advantage of me. They knew very well that there was something wrong with me. They gave me their belongings so they would have nothing in their rooms. I kept everything. So if the Germans caught me, they would have found all the material. I always accepted the risk. I did not care. I stuck all the papers in a straw mattress.

There were other things I hid also. For instance, there were those who went to camp for other crimes—let's say a French woman had something to do with a German. That was *Rassenschande,* which means "shame to the race." You were dirtying the Aryan race. The French woman would have to shave her hair, and the German would be sent to the front. The German or French or Polish women would be sent to the factory camp. So they had photos of their boyfriends, if they were in love. And I kept those, too.

One day the other prisoners got carrion, meat from dead animals lying in the fields. They also got some lamb that had died from sickness. So we cut it up and cooked it secretly in the night. I got my portion, too, along with a lot of stolen onions. An awful smell penetrated everything in the place. It was the smell of a cadaver. We threw the bones away in the outhouse toilets. I could not eat it at all because of the smell and threw away all that I had left. I vomited it up. Everybody else ate. They ate very happily because they were starving.

The Germans became scared of this smell, of some kind of disease. They were afraid, not because they were concerned about us being sick, but because they were afraid of getting typhoid themselves. The Gestapo came to check, beating us and calling us to the office. They could not find out anything from me or anybody.

The sabotage went on. Every day when the men loaded the boxes for the bombs on the trucks they would load them in such a way that every one of them would crack, so that when they got to the airport they would fall apart. But the Germans could not catch the saboteurs.

I was still with my "husband," although I never lived together with him. But whenever he wanted sex or something else from me, I refused and got beaten. I still did not say anything because I was afraid to say I was not his wife. In this camp, he was with the men, anyhow, and I was with the women. I thanked God that we were separated.

We would stand in line for food, the women apart from the men. I would always be the last one. Because people were hungry they would run like animals for a place to stand, and I was always the last one because I was afraid.

One day I met a fellow from Warsaw, from the Old Town. So many of those Warsaw Gentiles were fantastic, helping Jews wherever they were. The smugglers also came from that same part of town. The workers in the towns, especially from Warsaw, were far from ignorant. The peasants were ignorant, but the workers went to schools, read books. They would join the Socialist Party, and they would be very well informed. They did not have that hatred of the Jews and saw the Jews more as fellow citizens.

On Sunday the men were allowed to come dance with the women, to talk, and all the Polish people would dance polkas. One Sunday, this one man from Warsaw came over to me and said, "Tell me. You are acting too refined. May I speak to you?" So I took him to my room.

"I don't want to flirt with you," he said. "Don't misunderstand. I just want—as a good person—to tell you, you don't behave properly. You are not going to your *gymnasium* now." He had realized I was Jewish and had gone to a private school. "Don't behave this way. When you go for food, use the most vulgar curses in Polish. Then you will be a real Pole. You shouldn't speak the way you do. You have to use *'damn, damn it,'* everything. Curse!" I did as he said, speaking the filthiest Polish from that point on.

One day, I was working on the assembly line to make these boxes for bombs. The plywood went through the machine and I had to move the wood for a drying process. This day I noticed the *Meister* of the factory, the foreman, was not there, and I was sure there were no other Germans there.

There was a Russian woman beside me, or at least I thought she was Russian. Everyone had to wear a patch on their shirt to show their nationality. The Poles wore a patch with a yellow "P," the Russians wore a patch saying "OST," which means East. Ukrainians from the Soviet Union also wore the same "OST" patch. Many times you could not tell who was Ukrainian and who was Russian because they all sounded like Russians. Only by their actions would you know. The Russians had hateful eyes when they looked at the Germans. Ukrainians were always charmingly sweet and sang, *"Heil Hitler!"*

I could not speak Russian, but I could understand it, and Russians could understand Polish. So I told this Russian woman when I saw all the Germans were gone, "Hey, don't forget that you're working for the Germans. Take it easy." I stopped working. When I stopped, she could not work, and the whole assembly line came to a halt. There was silence. We stood there doing nothing. Then this woman said to me, "You have to work! Why are you doing nothing?" *I had made a mistake. She was Ukrainian!*

I did not answer her.

"Hey, why aren't you doing anything?"

"Because I don't want to," I said. "Don't forget that you're working for the Germans."

She ran out from the factory right to the office. She called the *Meister* and told him what I said. She was screaming in Ukrainian. They got a translator. Naturally, they talked to me. I said she was crazy, that I never spoke to her. I did not know Russian and she could not speak Polish. She did not know what she was talking about. I told the German engineer, who liked me and for whom I was making drawings, that he knew very well that I would never say such a thing.

Actually, he understood that I had said it. But he was from the old generation. The very old ones were not Nazis, probably, but they were afraid. He probably wanted to help, so he tried to make nothing of it. I figured that the story was finished, but it was not.

During the dancing on Sunday my friend from Warsaw came over to me and started to say, quietly, "I must help you. I can't stand that you should be a victim. I want you to survive. I was listening to somebody from the office and they are planning to take you and send you to some camp. They will catch you the day after tomorrow. They even have your train tickets ready for you. They are just waiting to see who is doing the sabotage. You better run. *You know why!"* which meant that he knew I was Jewish. When they caught me, it would be for more than sabotage.

"Don't think *maybe,"* he said. "You better run. Right away. Tonight!"

The man from Warsaw told me that the Germans had camps for people who had tuberculosis and other chronic diseases. These people were not good for the Germans because they had to feed them and give them medical care. No matter how little, they had to give something. For them that was an expense that took food away from the soldiers. They usually pretended to take them away for a cure and then would simply gas them. So the man from Warsaw told me the plan was for them to say that I was still sick and they would send me to a camp where I would be killed.

I went to my so-called husband and said to him, "We have to run away." He loved it. For him it was an adventure. For me it was suffering because it was terrible to be in the fields and forests. During the day, you had to hide yourself somewhere and sleep. The forests were full of runaways. It was very dangerous to be there. You could be shot anytime. And if they caught us … But he did not think twice. Everything was fine. Just run.

That night we took as much clothing as we could. In the very early dawn, we ran away.

ESCAPE

We walked and walked until we got to some train station. It was a small station, and the ticket agent was not too bright. I told you before that the Jews were calling Germans "the stupid ones." The Germans may have been very good organizers of dying, of working, of killing, but they were never very smart. The Gestapo could be faked by almost anybody, very easily faked. And their police were not overly bright either. French police you could not cheat, they would never believe you whatever you said. But the Germans believed you. They were gullible.

My husband got the tickets—we had some money. We got on the train going to Poland. Back to Poland. I did not like the idea, but there was nothing else to do. The train was going to the East.

We had two small valises. I told my husband we should separate. If they caught us, they should not catch us both. He agreed.

I was sitting on the train when, to my bad luck, some German officer returning to the Polish or Russian front from leave attached himself to me. He liked me. He talked and talked, trying to pick me up. I made believe that I did not like to talk, and I would not answer.

It was not entirely bad that he sat and talked to me, because to some extent that protected me from the other passengers. I was hungry, and I did want to eat something. He did not know I was running away. He knew nothing. He talked to me, and I said, *"Jah, Jah, Nein, Nein."* That was all. I barely answered because I was afraid that he would realize what kind of accent I had.

At one station, he took me to a restaurant and bought me a delicious dinner. He came back with me, talking very cavalier-like, a big gentleman, talking, talking, until we got to a station called Schwiebus. Schwiebus was the old frontier between Germany and Poland. A big part of Poland, up to Poznan, had already become a part of the new Germany.

Schwiebus was a small but important crossroad. On one side of the station, by the building, there were all the Gestapo, the police, *Wachtmeister,* the SS, everybody, checking papers. On the other side of the train there was just barbed wire and a possible way to get to the fields.

I had no papers. They would know right away I was a runaway. My husband was sitting far away, in between two trains. He looked at me through the window. When I saw all the Gestapo, I did not say a word, but I got up and opened the doors on the other side of the train. He threw out the valises and then we both jumped out. The Germans on the train looked at us, but discreetly, as if they were not really looking. They knew that something was wrong, and they understood we were runaways. They knew we had no right to be on the train, but they did not say a word. There were so many people running away, even Germans running away.

The German who had been talking to me, being such a gentleman and so on, he was big eyes and speechless. But he did not move, and he did nothing to stop me.

We jumped out, and my husband opened the barbed wire with his hands and pushed me through. That was my reason for being with that man. He was really strong. He was a peasant worker. He pushed me through the barbed wire with all my clothing torn and a little bit of my flesh scratched. I was lucky, I went through. Then he got through. The German police didn't see us. It was interesting that the people inside the train did not call the police. They did not call, and they did not look toward us, trying to see what we were doing. They did not do anything. In this way we had a chance to run, and we did.

We ran away, with torn clothing, marching through the fields. We started to hear singing from people working in the fields, so we ran into the forest. We ran through the forest until we finally got to a field of very tall wheat where people were working. These people came over to us. They were Ukrainians, but Polish Ukrainians who spoke Polish. There were some Poles, too. They asked us who we were and why we were there. At that time, the story was that we had run away because the Germans had beaten us up. They beat us up and we beat them back. We never mentioned Jew or Gentile or sabotage. Always a lie.

So they told us to stay there and at night they would come with good food. We were starved by then. Sure enough, that night they came with soup and pieces of fatty meat and fat and everything—it was so delicious! We were eating like pigs. After we finished, I gave them a letter to send to my mother.

We asked them where Posen was. Posen was the German name for Poznan, and, although it was already part of Germany, it was still a Polish town. I thought I might find some place to hide there. Actually, I was terribly worried because I was going back to Poland, where I could never really hide. My husband always said, "Don't worry, you will be with my mother." His plan was to go to Warsaw, and I would spend the war in his house. I knew that I would be his victim when I got there.

So far I was managing to keep him away. He would beat me up. I would cry. He would say he was sorry. We would make up as friends. It would go on like this, a fake marriage, no marriage.

Not far from Posen we stopped at a farm. The people there gave us delicious food. They let us get warm. They gave us two beds to sleep in. The next day they said we must go because they were close to the frontier. With so many people running away they had a lot of problems with the Gestapo and the SS coming and checking. So we could not stay too long. Not that they did not want us. They just could not keep us there.

We left to go to Posen. We did not know where to go because there were two arrows on the signpost. One was left to Posen and the other was right to Posen. We did not know which was correct. We stopped a fellow who was tending cows in the fields and asked him in Polish. Maybe he was a *Volksdeutscher*. Sure enough, he gave us directions right to the police.

When we started to walk we realized we had made a mistake. There were police on horseback, big fat Germans in uniforms, who started to run after us, yelling, "Stop! Stop!" We ran in between the houses to hide. After half an hour I knew we had no chance. The Polish people—peasants—sat in their houses. They did not budge. They did not move outside to help the police. They just sat inside while we were running between the houses. Finally, the police shouted, "Stop or we'll shoot!" So we stopped. But we had been chased for quite a long time before we did.

PRISON

We were arrested and sent to prison in Wroclaw. It was a prison for men, and Marian was put with the men. One cell was empty, so they put me there. Sure enough, soon I was sharing it with another Jewish girl. She was caught as a Jewess. I was terribly worried because they never put Jews together with Gentiles. And not with a German, that was for sure. If there was another German, they kept him in a separate cell. Otherwise it would be *Rassenschande,* "dirtying the race," just by touching.

So I wondered why they kept me with her. I was afraid that maybe my "husband" had squealed. I was plenty worried.

I was always saying Catholic prayers, always praying in front of this girl. I thought maybe she was planted as a Gestapo helper. Funniest thing was she would say to me, "Start saying your prayers." And I would say, "Why?" Actually, it seemed she did not know how to pray. But I was not sure if she really did know and was simply checking, or if she did not know and was afraid.

She told me she was from Lodz. She did not say she was Jewish, and I never asked. That was one thing we could never speak about. Nobody ever spoke of their real problems, because if we were beaten we would sing.

As the days went by I found out she was very sick with tuberculosis. "If you survive the war," she told me, "my name is Nawaroska. Remember to announce that in the papers so my family will know what happened. I cannot survive. I am very sick and I will kill myself anyhow."

I had long hair tied in a knot at the back. I had razor

blades hidden in the knot in order to commit suicide in case I could not take it anymore. She begged me to give her one, but I did not want to. I felt that if she committed suicide, it would be my fault that she killed herself. After a while they took her away, I do not know where. They seemed to know she was Jewish. They did not know about me.

When we were arrested, they asked me about myself, what we were doing. "We weren't running away," I said. "We were lost from the transport of workers to Germany." I always gave them the same story—that we had been marching and marching and did not know what to do, so we started to go back home. The investigator was an Austrian. He spoke very softly to me, very nicely, charmingly. One thing I never forgot was the good advice of the Gentile engineer from Warsaw: "No matter what, if they are good or bad, you can never trust Germans. Whatever they say, it is only to get to the truth—so you must always lie. Never admit a thing." With Doctor Klein I took a chance because he showed that he had such a good heart that I felt I could tell him the truth. He was the exception.

The investigator even said to me, "Look, you can speak to me. I am Austrian. I am not German. I hate the Germans. I know sooner or later we will lose the war. I am on your side. You can tell me. Why are you running away?"

"Why are you putting things in my mouth? I don't know what you're talking about. I was not running away."

"Tell me the truth," he laughed. "I won't do anything to you."

I never admitted anything, so they kept me in that prison.

Meanwhile, there was one prisoner who was the trustee of that ward of the prison, a Polish fellow whose job it was to serve the other prisoners their meals. Whenever I got food, he would make it very thick with meat so that I should eat plenty. The other girl, Nawaroska, while she was still with me, would not even touch her food. "Eat my food, too," she would tell me. "It is my way of committing suicide." She had decided to stop eating. She did not want to touch the food, but I was very hungry and ate.

They would take me to the office in the prison. I pretended that I did not speak German. Whenever they questioned me, they had a translator, a Gentile Polish fellow, I did not know if he was a *Volksdeutscher* or not. They were asking my name. The Austrian would ask more questions. The translator helped me with his eyes. When I was not to answer, he would cover his mouth that I should not answer. He was helpful.

After a few days there, they sent me from the prison chained to a group of men. We were all tied together with iron chains, and we were marched to the train to be sent back to Germany. As we were marched down the street in chains, I saw on the sidewalk right next to us the Ukrainian who was one of the owners of the brushmakers' factory in Warsaw. I got such a fright. He was the only one who could identify me as a Jew, if he saw me. Quickly, I turned my face away, and we passed.

The people at the train station looked at us as if we were terrible criminals, killers. But we were all prisoners for political reasons, for sabotage, or for saying something against Germany or Hitler. All the time I was in prison in Germany, I never met anybody who was actually a thief or a bandit or a criminal. I only found people in there for reasons like "insulting the race," things like that. As a matter of fact, I never met criminals even amongst the German prisoners. I had a chance to be with German prisoners—we were separated, but I had a chance to hear what they said because we marched together.

I was taken with my "husband" to a place where they kept prisoners who were being sent back to work or to a camp. Again the same thing happened to me that had hap-

pened at the detention camp in Warsaw. A woman came over
to me who said she was in prison because she was a fortune-
teller. She took my hand and, just like the palm reader in
Warsaw, she was scared by what she saw. Again, death,
suffering, beatings. "You might survive, or you might not."
She told me the most terrible things.

We slept there a few days. Very early each morning,
around four o'clock, they would call and give us artificial
coffee. One night I dreamt that I saw my dead father. He
was very weak and covered with snow. Snow was falling all
around him. I woke up and went to this fortune-teller in the
middle of the night. I woke her up and asked her what this
dream meant.

"Today," she said to me, "when they call for coffee, they
will call your name. The Gestapo will talk to you, the first to
be questioned. There will be two men. Or three. One man
will be a very good man. And one man will try to fix you up
so that you go to a camp to be killed. They will fight between each other. Be smart. Answer carefully. Make believe
you don't understand, but then listen to what they say so
you can understand what is happening in the interrogation.
You will not be set free. You will be sent back to Germany to
do forced labor. You will not go to the camp."

It happened exactly as she said. This was unbelievable.
She really said exactly what happened. I got coffee. Soon
after that, they called me along with two other people. I was
the first to be interrogated. There were two men. One spoke
German, and I said I did not understand. They got somebody to translate, so then there were three. In the meantime,
I had a chance to hear what they were saying to each other.

"She surely did something," one of them said. "She ran
away."

"What do you care?" the other one replied. "If she says
she wants to go to work, that's all we need. We need workers."

They began asking questions. "What's your name? What

is this or what is that?" I was trying to figure out what to say and then think, and I answered mostly that I did not understand. I did not say much. I was concerned that they might ask too many questions. I simply said I wanted to go to work. Why don't they send me to work?

They sent us to a prison in Berlin, near the *Bahnhoff,* the train station. The women were completely separated from the men. There I met a French woman who was a princess, a countess, or a baroness, I'm not sure which. She had been married to a Jewish fellow but then divorced him. Yet never during the war did she give him away. He was with the *maquis,* the French underground. She herself had a radio station and had sent news to England. They caught her, and they wanted to find out about her husband, but she would not give him away.

She was my biggest friend in Berlin. We walked together when they gave us time for walking around the courtyard. She did not know I was Jewish. She ended up being sent to an awful camp, Ravensbruck, where she almost lost her life. It was by sheer luck she survived. They kept her as a hostage, in case they wanted to exchange her for other prisoners. She survived and I met her later after the war in Paris.

It is interesting that I always encountered good Germans. In this courtyard we could walk or march or run, whatever we felt like. The police watched us from all sides. There was one policeman, extremely handsome and young, who, when we passed by, looked over and pushed something to me and the French woman. We were his favorites. I do not know why. It was a big package—his lunch. He gave it away. There were two big apples and a sandwich, so we split it and ate it together. He left a card inside with a note: "Make believe you are sick. Go to the prison hospital. There you will get good soup to eat." So we did that and every day we would get good soup to eat. One day he disappeared. They took him away from guard duty because one of the women noticed he was being friendly with us. I do not know what happened to him.

There was bombing day and night. We slept through it. I cared nothing about the bombing. I was not really scared. I did not even react. When they called us down to the cellars, which were like catacombs inside, I did not even want to go down. One night I was sleeping in my bunk, when this Zosia—another Zosia, from Lodz, a twisted, bow-legged, crazy Gentile girl who was a lesbian—came to me and started touching me. When she touched me I did not even wake up, but I felt it. I gave her a push. I was in the fourth or fifth bunk, and she fell down and hurt herself. She started to scream. After that, she went to one of the women police guards and denounced me.

While I was in prison I always prayed regular Catholic prayers, not because I wanted to pray, but because it was forbidden. Prayers were not allowed. It was against Hitler. Prayers were like communism, not allowed. National songs, not allowed. Anything against Germany, definitely not. I would do everything possible to start the morning with a national song. All day I would sing Christmas carols or songs about Poland. I sang songs like, "Here's the enemy of humanity, Hitler. He's a devil. He will pass. God will triumph. We will go back to the country. We will throw out the Germans. We will throw out the Russians. We will throw out everybody. We will be free again."

So I sang, and this Zosia knew I was the leader. I was like a priestess. It was for a selfish reason, my doing that. I wanted to stir the Polish people up against the Germans at all costs. I wanted them to remember who their enemy was and that they should not comply. So wherever I was, I used sabotage, prayers, and national songs to stir them up. And the Polish people were stirred up easily with Polish or religious songs.

So when this Zosia went to the *Wachtmeister* and said,

"She's the one! She's the one who is singing songs! She is praying!" they put me in isolation in the catacombs, a dungeon, for two days and two nights. I said to myself, "Oh, my God. When I get out, I will beat her up."

There was some kind of disease in the men's section of the prison, and the Germans got so scared they decided to send the women away, deeper into Germany, away from Berlin. The next day a bomb—Russian, English, or American—fell on the prison and many were killed. It was just one day after I had left. We got this news from hearing the policemen talking, saying, "Thank God we were sent out!" But thank God the prisoners were sent out! The women of Bahnhoff Prison were saved! Since my "husband" was still in the prison, I didn't know if he survived or not.

I was taken to Frankfurt. I think there are two Frankfurts, but I do not know which I was sent to. Everybody was normally allowed to be loose in a compartment on the train. But me? No. There was a separate compartment enclosed by iron bars for special prisoners, dangerous prisoners. I could not sit down, only stand. If there had been an accident on that train I would never have gotten out. I would have burned. The train was closed in for prisoners, but I was extra closed in.

When I got to Frankfurt, I was put in a cell where there was already a Polish girl from Warsaw. She was brunette. She did not have that typical Polish turned-up nose and blond hair and blue eyes. No, she was darkish. We could have been cousins, but she was not Jewish.

She started to talk about life before the war. I happened to know certain famous actors since I had been going to the artists' clubs, having a good time with the cream of the youth. Playing and dancing, always with the best. She happened to be from the same café society. She started to talk. One thing led to another. "I think you are the one," she said, "who was beaten up by that Zosia from Lodz."

"Yes," I said. "I was sent to the dungeon, not beaten, but put in the dungeon."

Later she started to knock on our cell door to get people's attention. Other prisoners came by when they heard her. She was a leader in that prison. She talked with them about this woman, Zosia. When we were allowed out in the courtyard, right away these women threw some kind of rag over Zosia and she got beaten to a pulp. She did not know who was beating her. Zosia got beaten for denouncing—so that she should know a Pole does not denounce, that she should never denounce anybody, and she should remember it forever and ever.

Eventually, I was assigned to work on a farm and left this prison.

PROHNO'S FARM

The overseer of the farm was named Prohno. He was a very big guy, and a real Nazi, very mean, very sadistic. I lived in a house with the families of farmers from Poland. In the room next to mine was a Ukrainian from Poland who was a teacher. He was always trying to find out things, maybe collaborating with the Germans. In the meantime, he gave me books and I started to study Ukrainian.

I was sick with hepatitis for the entire year. What they fed me was not good for hepatitis. I never had meat. I had ration cards for a piece of fat, but I changed it for sugar, which I thought was good for me. I would lie in bed whenever I could. My whole body was dead yellow, but I would still work.

Finally, I got so bad they sent me to a German doctor. I had to walk there. I waited in his office for hours until finally he took me. He was a real good Nazi, this doctor. He did not want to see me when it was my turn, and made me wait. He just wanted me to suffer.

When I went into his office, he showed me a map—very strange behavior for a doctor—and he asked, "Where do you come from?" By that time I spoke fluent German, and I was not in the hands of the Gestapo. I said I was from Polesie, close to the frontier with Russia. I figured the Russians were fighting with the Germans and would take the town over and the Germans would not be able to check on whether or not I was telling the truth. I did not admit I was from Warsaw.

"You are from there?" he said. "All these Jews, these Poles and Jews, they should die. They should all be killed. I don't know why we are using them as workers."

"You are very sick," he then said. "You think I will give you medicine? You are very much mistaken. We need medicine for our soldiers, for our Germans. For foreigners—for Poles and Jews—nothing! The Poles, the Russians, and the Jews—nothing!"

I walked out. I found some kind of pen. I wrote on the wall in German, "DROP DEAD HITLER AND YOU WITH HIM!" I did not sign it. I did not know if he would know it was me, but I left my mark. I was so sick I could barely walk anymore, but I walked back to the farmhouse anyway.

A little German woman who worked in the office started coming to my room. I found out later that she was the sweetheart of this overseer, Prohno. He had a wife, a big fat woman, very tall and very mean. Once, during a bombing, a big plane crashed, an American plane. During the night, the farmers—mostly Polish—went and made braided flowers, a wreath, and put it on the remains of the bodies. But during the day, Prohno's wife went there to dig out the eyes of one of the victim's heads, cutting off the ears. The parts were all over—a hand here, a leg there, a head, the tags with their names, a Bible. We all felt terrible about it. In any case, Prohno's sweetheart would come to visit me, bringing me food and asking how I was, always telling me I would survive.

I stayed a long time in bed. I do not know by what miracle I did not die, but after a long time the hepatitis passed, and I went back to work.

I never knew how to milk a cow. I lied that I knew how to milk cows. But by this time I had learned farm work, although I did not have strength to do much. All the tools were very heavy. One day they were putting natural fertilizer—manure—on a cart and I could not lift it. It was already winter and the manure was frozen. There was a Polish couple who had a very funny name, Hujka, which sounds almost like "a man's organ" in Polish. So they came over to help. If they hadn't, the whole cart would have fallen over.

There was a *Volksdeutscher* family who shouted, "Why are you helping this Jewess?" One thing led to another. They started to beat each other with pitchforks until they bled. Soon enough the police came. They came to my room to try to find out why the other workers had been beating each other. "I don't know," I said.

There was another incident. My so-called "husband" had survived the bombing of the prison in Berlin, and he had told the Germans that he wanted to work with his wife. So he had joined up with me again, and he was furious that I still kept him at a distance. One day we were fighting. He took a knife that he had hidden and cut my face. For a very long time I had a scar on my face—it took ten years to disappear. They tried to check him, too. But I could never say the truth. I would just suffer and accept it.

Once, Teresa Koschmider came to visit me, the woman I had known in the prison hospital in Gronau who gave me a Bible and told me about the Warsaw Ghetto uprising. She had run away. We had been writing letters to each other. She stayed in my room for a day and then she had to move on because I could not keep her. I gave her a little bit to eat and she left. I never saw her again.

Things were getting hot around there. I knew something was wrong. The other farm workers talked about me. They never told me anything, and they would never tell Marian anything either, but they suspected that I was Jewish. When I had been sick with hepatitis, this Hujka woman had come over to me one day. I was wearing a cross, naturally. She said, "You know, the Jews in Poland came to cheat us. They said, 'You buy this, you buy that,' and they cheated us all the time." As she talked she kept hitting me while I lay in bed. It hurt me terribly. She wanted to hear me scream, *"Oy vay!"* or something. I tried to hold on despite the pain. She and her husband helped me with the work, but they were anti-Semitic nonetheless. Still, they didn't want to give me away and have me killed. They probably couldn't bring themselves to do it. They did not love Jews, but they hated Germans more.

I was working in the fields one day. It was winter and I was not working well. This German, Prohno, saw how poorly I was working. He said to me, *"Willst du Klavier spielen?* Would you like to play the piano rather than work?" He was laughing at me. Then he decided I could be put to better use somewhere else. If I was not good for the fields, I would have to change my work. He had a *Volksdeutscher* woman who worked in the kitchen, but she was stealing too much food. Everybody stole food. It was a question of survival. But she was stealing too much, so he decided to send her to the fields and put me in the kitchen.

In the kitchen I ate better, stealing only a little food for myself since I had no family to steal for. I was careful because I knew why they had thrown the other woman out. But this woman did not want to admit to herself that she had been stealing too much and the Germans had noticed it. She decided to give me away as a Jewess. She went to Prohno and said something.

Prohno locked me in my room. I was not allowed to go out. Mrs. Hujka passed me news and some food through the window. After a few days, Prohno called me to the office. He had an office connected to a brewery where the German workers made beer. He simply took a stick and started beating me on the head and shoulders. "Who are you? Who are you?" he shouted as he beat me.

I said, "I'm Polish!" in German.

"You are not Polish! Who are you?" He beat me without stopping. The German workers in the brewery knew that he was beating me. They just wrung their hands, disgusted. They could not stand that he was beating me like this.

All of a sudden, I reminded myself of what the Gentile engineer had advised me: Never admit anything if they beat you. As a matter of fact, if a German beats you up and you don't fight back, that means you are a Jew, that you are scared. A Gentile always strikes back. Whenever a German attacked Polish people, the Poles would take it until they could not stand it anymore and then they would kill the German.

I was already bleeding and dizzy, but it came to my mind that I had to hit back. I had these wooden shoes. As little as I was—and he was a big man—I kicked him right in his organ. He was in terrific pain. He started to holler. Then he took one of the hunting rifles from the wall and stuck it against my belly. He wanted to shoot me because I had hit him.

At that moment, his mistress, the little woman who used to visit me, came in and said to him, "Don't! Don't kill her!"

Meanwhile, his wife, the big fatso, also came in and screamed, "Shoot her! Shoot her!"

It was a question of who would win his heart. Well, the sweetheart won.

"Don't shoot her," she repeated. "We are close to the end of the war. A time will come when we will have to answer for our crimes. Don't shoot her. Don't shoot her." And he threw the rifle away.

He called one of his men from the brewery. "Take them both, the husband along with the wife, and send them somewhere," he told him. I did not know where he would take us, and I was worried. We were near the Black Forest, and somewhere nearby there was a work camp where they kept all kinds of nationalities. They would check who they were as they arrived, then send them on to hard labor camps. In a week or ten days everybody died in those camps. Past two weeks hardly anyone survived. It was work without stop, day and night, beatings without stop. These were terrible camps. If somebody came out after two weeks, they had to have a strong physical constitution and mental strength.

We were sent to another camp. A German from the brewery was to take the train with us. Before we got on the train we stopped in the fields by the station. "I am telling you while no one can hear us," he said. "I am going to the station to buy tickets. If I lose them, no one will know. You run away. I won't see anything. When I come back with the tickets, you will not be here."

At that point we were so scared we did not know what to do. We were both disoriented. We did not know how or what or where to go. We did not know exactly what part of Germany we were in. We did not have courage for the moment. With all the ordeal, we were exhausted. We could not do it.

"You stupid idiots!" he said when he came back and we were still there. He was disgusted that we were there waiting for him.

He took us on to the train. There were some seats. "Sit down," he told me while he stood. Some of the Germans said, "What's this? Why give a foreigner a seat while you are standing?"

"She is more tired than I am," he said. "I'm sure she has been working harder than I have. She is working for us. Leave her alone."

They started to holler, and this man got into a big fight. There were Nazis on the train. And there were people against the Nazis. All of a sudden they started to argue. One Nazi said he would stop the train to give them all away.

"You can give us away," some man said. "It's almost the end of the war. You will be killed. And I tell you what, you will be the first to be killed!"

"Give me your name," the other one said.

"I won't give you my name."

The Germans were starting to talk. Before they would only say *"Heil Hitler!"* and nothing else. Now they were starting to talk, and they were less and less afraid to be critical.

As the train approached the next station, the ones who were saying the war was almost over and Hitler would lose got up and ran away. They would not go any farther on that train. They got scared. The others stayed.

"DO YOU LIKE GERMANS?"

We got to the camp in the Black Forest. It was a very big camp. They put me in with the Polish women, and my "husband" was taken to the men. They did not have a job for me. They did not know where to put me to work. But somebody had to check on me. They did not take me there just to work. They wanted to find out who I was.

They took me to the office. On the desk were the papers they had about me, and I glanced at them. There was a big black cross, which meant dangerous prisoner. A Gestapo man asked me a lot of questions, and I answered in German. He did not beat me, just asked me questions. He said, "Tell everything, the truth. You will be very well treated. As a matter of fact, you will be sent to the barracks with the German women where you will get better treatment. But you must tell the truth."

They never put the Poles with the Germans. It was a lie. I knew when he said this that it was some kind of trick. It could not be the truth because it would be *Rassenschande,* dirtying the race, even to mix the women.

He asked where I came from, the name of my parents. I said that I was an orphan. I did not know my parents at all. He asked what I did before the war. I said I worked as a maid. I worked for the Jews and the Gentiles.

He asked a lot of things. "Do you like Pilsudski?" I said, "I did." This could mean two things. Either I was a Jew, because Jews liked Pilsudski, or I was pro-German. Pilsudski had made believe that he was with the Germans against the Russians because he wanted the independence of Poland. He did not like Germans. As a matter of fact, he hated them all. He only wanted Poland to be independent. But in

Poland to like Pilsudski had meant to be pro-German. So the Gestapo man was kinder to me.

"Do you like Germans?" he asked. I did not answer right away. I thought about the question for quite a while. I did not know what to answer. I thought like this: If you say that you do not like them, then you would be telling the truth. But why don't you like them, that is the point. Are you Jewish or are you Polish? I decided that the truth is the best lie.

"I don't like the Germans," I said.

"Yes, but your papers say you came willingly to work."

"Yes, I came willingly, but I do not like the Germans for one thing only. I like them in principle, but I don't like that they came and took over Poland. Otherwise I don't have anything against the Germans. They work beautifully. They don't like the Jews. That's fine with me." Naturally, it was important to keep saying everything I could against the Jews.

"These papers don't look real to me." Then he told the truth, curiously enough. "There was a woman who said very bad things about you." It was the *Volksdeutscher* woman who was working in the kitchen who I'd replaced and who had denounced me. I knew what she had said, that I was Jewish. "But we will check your papers. We will check the town in Poland."

I thought to myself, how could he check the town? The Russians had taken it over. I found out much later that the Germans were still there and the Russians had not come yet.

"However, I don't see anything wrong right now. Don't worry. We will move you to another camp. You go to work—and you better work fast!"

They put me to work for the army. We made screws and parts for the planes and tanks. They showed me how, and in a very short time I was working very well. In this camp everybody worked in big halls. While they worked, they were free to move around, go to the toilet. But not me. A policeman sat behind me all the time. When I went to the bathroom, he went with me and stood outside the door. I was never free to move around. When the work was finished, he took me back to the camp. I was never free for a moment. He would watch how I worked—and I worked very fast.

Then the Yugoslavs came over to me, and the Czechs, all the nationalities. They would pass by and say to me, "Watch out! We will kill you. Don't forget you are working for the Germans." They spoke in their own languages, not German, so the guard would not understand. The Germans understood English and a little French, but not the other languages. When it came to the Slavic languages, they were all lost. The workers would pass by, and I would answer, "I cannot help myself. You can help. You stop working. You work slow!"

So I would work slow, and then the German would say that I must work fast. So I worked fast. Then I would slow down. Then he would make me go fast. I was driven crazy.

Then one day I was working very fast with these screws on the machine, filing and measuring the exact size, not spoiling them. I was scared; they were checking me so much. They would know immediately if I did something wrong. That day this guard looked at me in a funny way. He was an older man, and as I've pointed out, the older Germans were not Nazis or they often felt sorry for the people they were guarding. He was more human.

The guard was sitting, and he said, "Your papers are very bad. This time when I take you, you will not work anymore. Do you understand? You are not going to work anymore. You try to do whatever you think is right. You know what I mean."

He did not say to run away. It was a very difficult matter to run away. The camp was enclosed with walls. The rest of the day was a holiday, and they gave us free time. I had a chance to check the camp all over. There was a farm with Polish people right next to the camp. That would be my exit.

Later, the guard spoke to me again. "You are going," he said, "to the German barracks." At the same time that he said this, his head was showing me no, that this was not true. "Here is a canteen for food," he said. "Whatever ration cards you have, get yourself everything you can take, whatever you can use, like bread or salami. Get everything."

I went to the store. When I walked out he was waiting, but I could not run away. It was impossible. I thought of how I could run away when all of a sudden the German looked in the other direction. A jeep with the SS in their black uniforms was coming.

Black uniforms meant death. When the black uniforms came, that was when they would take people. In Germany, as I've said, there was a law that they had to beat you until they found out who you were. Then when you admitted, they would hang you with your head upside down so that you died by your own blood. Or they would start a fire or torture you if you were a Jew. They would not bother sending you to a camp. When they wanted to commit anything illegal in Germany, they would send the SS in their black uniforms. They would take you under some pretext and you would be shot. When I saw this jeep with the black uniforms, with their hats with skeleton heads and the SS, I knew this was my end.

I said to the man, "I have to get my clothing." I did not tell him the truth, and he knew that I was lying. He knew very well where my barracks were, but I headed to the men's camp. I wanted to get their help. I knew there were some from Warsaw who I was sure would help me. Many people were running away from this camp.

I got to the men's camp right at lunchtime. When I ran in somebody said, "That's the Jewess! That's the Jewess from Warsaw!" They immediately threw a sack on him, so he would not know who did it, and they beat him up good. They brought me my valise from the women's camp. They told my "husband" that he should take his things. They turned around, looking away while I put on a lot of clothing, as much as I could manage. They gave us some vodka and said, "Run!" We ran toward the farm. We did not know if the Germans were looking for us or if we had enough time, but we ran away to this farm that was right next to the camp.

THE BLACK FOREST

We ran to the farmhouse where Polish people were living. When they came back from the fields we told them that we ran away because we beat up a German.

"Oh, you beat up a German? Oh, my God!" they exclaimed. They put us up in the attic. Then we heard the police running with the dogs. They were looking around the forest with the dogs. But they did not find us. I did not understand, because the dogs should have smelled our scent. But somehow they did not find us.

We waited. We asked the Polish people for food and left them almost all the ration tickets we had. They gave us whatever they could, all that we could carry, and we ran into the mountains of the Black Forest. We made a mistake at first and ended up back at the same place where we had started. But we were scared and just kept running.

We saw some people on a picnic. They did not even look at us. They were not interested, and we ran away. It was getting dark. We tried to figure out where we were. Lights from the town were far away, so we knew that we had already traveled enough.

We marched and marched and marched. Then we finished all the food. We walked at night and hid during the day. We were trying to go to Switzerland. We did not have a map or a compass to guide ourselves by. But I would look at the trunks of the trees. Where there was moss, it was north. The opposite was south, and I could tell which way was east and west. I knew that if we went toward the west we would go to Switzerland. South would be France.

One night we were walking when all of a sudden we heard heavy breathing all around us. An army was marching.

We heard the quiet metal sounds of their gear, their knapsacks. They were marching, but it was such a pitch dark night we did not even know we were walking between the soldiers of an army. We stopped walking, frozen. We were lucky that nobody touched us. They probably had orders to march quietly. They never saw us, and we never saw them either. But we heard them.

It was terrible running away. There was constant rain. There were bicycles along the road we could have used, but my mother had never let me learn how to ride one, nor did she let me learn how to swim. We got to some river. Marian knew how to swim, but he could not leave me because I did not know how to get across. There was a bridge. A German was under the bridge marching back and forth on guard duty. So we went over the bridge. Quietly, whenever he put down his foot, we put down our feet. I had these wooden shoes with linen on top, but I could not wear them. I walked barefoot because they would have made too much noise.

Then we marched in terrific rainstorms. It was hot rain because it was summer. There were many people who ran away into the forests. There were some English troops, some parachutists, some Russians, Americans. There were all kinds of people there—Poles, escaped French prisoners of war. But there were no Jews.

We were getting weak from hunger. I smelled some bushes. They smelled like chicken, like roasted chicken. I started to eat the leaves. I had to spit them out—this was not chicken! However, I knew mushrooms very well. We used to go to the country a lot before the war and I knew which mushrooms were good. We picked mushrooms and we peeled the skin from them, eating them raw, being very careful to not get poisoned. We did not have water either. What water we could get was full of frogs and tadpoles, disgusting water.

We would find onions from the fields and gardens. It was then I realized who this "husband" of mine really was.

He was a plain thief. For him to steal, to go to somebody's house to steal clothing or a chicken, was nothing. He lived on stealing. He would go at night to rob farmers. He mostly got onions from vegetable gardens. We lived on whatever he could steal. We found some potatoes that had been left behind in the fields after harvest. We cleaned them with our hands.

But it was mainly onions that we ate. I ate so many onions my perspiration smelled of onions. I smelled of onions for two or three months. All the cells of my body were penetrated with onions. That was the main food we got. If not for that, we probably would have died. Onions are quite nourishing. It was not too bad.

Then my "husband" got an idea. "We're near a town," he said. "You have to go to the bakery and get bread."

"No," I told him. "You go." But he was dressed so funny. He did not even have a man's shirt on. He was wearing my blouse. Right away he would have looked suspicious, wearing a woman's blouse with his pants, so he could not go. I had normal clothing, only I was very dirty. So I cleaned myself in the stream water. I went to the village. I gave the baker some ration cards that we had. But before he gave me the bread, the baker asked, "Where do you come from? Where are you working?" He could tell I was a farm worker, so he figured I worked somewhere nearby.

"With Mueller," I said. In Germany every other name is Mueller or Miller.

"Oh, with Mueller, fine, fine!" He put the bread in a bag—and it was a big one—and gave it to me and took the coupons. Then this dumbbell, as soon as he gave me the bread, he started to think, "With Mueller? She looks so dirty." Then he started to think I didn't look normal. If I was working with some German family, I would have had clean clothing. I would look clean. Working on a farm we never got soap, but we would get a chance to wash up. We would not have looked like runaways who lived in the forest. So he started to think, then he started to run after me. But by then I had run into the forest.

When I got back to my "husband," he grabbed the bread. He ate the whole thing, practically giving me nothing.

We got to the point that we were thinking of committing suicide simply because we could not go any farther. We did not know where we were, marching only at night. During the day people worked in the fields. On the roads there were trucks and bicycles, maybe soldiers, police. We could not walk during the day. How long could we have lived like that?

Once, we climbed into a haystack to sleep, and the next morning when we woke up there were people working in the field around us. We had not realized that in the night. It looked like it was near the forest. But we fell asleep with the little field mice. Hay and straw make you sleepy. In fact, you can die if you breathe that air long enough, the air filled with carbon dioxide. When I woke up, I felt hot, but my feet were cold. "Why are my feet cold," I thought, "when I am so hot in the straw?" My legs were completely sticking out of the haystack. And the haystack was right by the road where all the bikes were passing by. I jumped out and the haystack fell apart.

Then we ran between the wheat, hiding, and we got to a place where the wheat was extremely high. There we began to hear Polish songs. I said these must be prisoners of war or something. "They are Polish and perhaps they will help us." When they sang, we answered their songs.

"Who's there? What are you doing here?" they asked after they saw us. At this time I had another, a stronger, story. "I killed a German," I told them.

When they heard that, they got so panicked they had no words. They were prostrate from fear. There was only one thing to do. They would bring us food at night.

At that time I wrote a letter to my mother in Krakow. I wrote: "Dear Mrs. Dimka. Please don't write to me anymore at my old address because I left there. Where I am going I don't know. Maybe after the family stops beating each other (which meant when the war was over) then I will let you know. But, please, after you get this don't try to write to me anymore." I did not want her to get caught. That's all that was on my mind.

I gave the letter to somebody who passed it from one family to another, from one Pole to another, until it was finally sent out from ten villages away, so no one would know where it came from. How they did that I don't know, but she got the letter, as I found out later.

The Polish farmworkers said we could not stay. They had already helped some other people and they were being watched. They told us to go two or three villages farther, then simply go to the police and say that we got lost from the transport of workers and we want to work in Germany. Yes, we knew that story.

I discussed this with Marian. Then I said, "This is the time to tell them the truth. We have to tell the truth. If they ask you or beat you, what will you say?"

"I will tell them you are Jewish."

"Marvelous," I said. "Just go ahead and do it. And I'll tell you what I'll do. If they ask me if it is true, you know what I will say? That you took me from Warsaw, from the ghetto, and you brought me here."

Helping Jews meant the death penalty. He was not supposed to save Jews. When he heard that he said, "Oh, Maria, what will I do now? This Jewess has a good head. I am really fixed up."

"Don't start with me," I said. "You are in trouble. I am in trouble. We are running away. We've suffered together. But you don't have to turn against me. Let's finish this war peacefully and don't give me away. If you give me away, I will give you away. And I will even give them the address of your mother so they will pick her up in Warsaw, too!"

So he began to reconsider. He could not say much. But

I had my second thoughts, too. I decided I would not say that he helped me as a Jewess. If he said nothing and I came out with that, it was no good for me. But I could say one thing which was true—that he was not my husband. That way, if I came out alive from the interrogation, I would be separated from him for good. That was what I wanted. He would not know. The Gestapo did not repeat what you said when you squealed. They would only repeat something when they wanted to confront you with it.

So we went up to a policeman in some village and told him our story. While he listened he had a terrific idea. He said, "Oh, poor children. You like Germans? We have to help you. I have a very good idea. I'll take you to my house. You can be my maid, and he can help me in the garden. And I won't tell anybody!"

But his wife told him immediately that he could not do that. He was a policeman, he had to turn us in. We could not be in his house. "You cannot keep them until the end of the war. You have to take them to the station." They gave us food, and we washed ourselves and worked a little bit. But they had to get rid of us, so he took us to the police station.

I made believe that I did not speak German. There was a Polish man who was the translator. My hair was fixed up with a lot of little braids to make me look like a peasant. Before I was interrogated, this translator took one look at me and said, "No normal Polish girl would comb her hair like this. Better straighten your hair and look normal. Don't try to be someone you're not. I'm just giving you a warning. This does not look good on you."

At the station the policeman told us to stand in one corner of the room because we smelled so much of onions. Then the Germans asked us our story. I told the story to the Polish man first so he could translate to the Germans. He listened to our story. "I like that. It's a good story," he told me. He did not believe a word. Then he translated it for the gullible Germans.

THE GESTAPO JAIL

Then we got sent to a real prison, and I was put in a small cell with maybe twenty other women. There was one Russian girl, a French girl from Paris, and one Polish girl, a worker from Warsaw. There were Ukrainians, all types of people, but there were no Jews in the cell, although there were some Jews in the prison, on the other side.

There were two sisters, German Jewish girls, whose father was a Gentile and whose mother was Jewish. The father was in the Nazi party, so he divorced his wife, acting as if he did not want her. But he did it to save his daughters. He was trying to be the biggest Nazi possible. He used his influence, his friends and so on, just to keep them in prison until the end of the war. He was willing to do anything to keep them from going to a camp, from being killed, so he kept them safe in prison. One of the girls was very beautiful. The other was very ugly. I had a feeling that the ugly one hated me.

There was one day of the week, Wednesday, that the Gestapo made their decision about who would stay and who would go. That was our court, the day when the Gestapo decided. Some prisoners were sent to a hard labor camp for two weeks, or to another kind of labor camp, which was a little bit easier. Or some would be sent to freedom which just meant going back to forced labor. But at least it was not a camp. At nighttime, you were free to walk around if you wanted. You worked holidays without pay. On Sunday you were not allowed to go to church. You were not allowed to travel from one village to another. Only Ukrainians had this right because they were pro-German. But at least forced labor was freedom of a sort.

So there were certain days when we knew that a person would be sentenced to a camp. If you were not called by the Gestapo that day, you were sent to offices to clean floors, to wash windows, things like that. When we washed windows or floors, we would get extra soup. One day I got extra soup from the *Wachtmeister,* the guard, who was an older man, a very nice man, who gave extra food to whoever cleaned offices. We got acquainted. He asked what I used to do. I said I liked to draw. So he showed me photos of his family, and I made a drawing for him. He loved that drawing so much that he did not have words to thank me.

One day I was washing windows. There was a big cell with many men and I wanted to go to that cell. I had heard that a little Englishman was there. The Englishman was a little tiny blond fellow who had parachuted, for what reason I did not know. He flew with the English Air Force. He had parachuted and had gotten caught. They questioned him, but he would not say what he was supposed to be doing. He would not say his name. He would say nothing but "England!" They asked him many questions and he never said anything. He was sentenced to be killed.

That day I brought him a little soup under some pretext. I said a few words to him in English, and he welcomed me.

"Who are you?" I asked.

"I am English. I am going to be killed."

"Your family knows where you are?" I asked.

"I cannot even tell you my name. I can only tell you I am English and I parachuted."

He was so courageous. Tears would not even come from his eyes. Or he was so depressed that he could not cry. I do not know what happened. I never saw him after that. It could be they shot him in the courtyard.

Then the Gestapo started to ask me questions, bringing me in for interrogations, asking me who I was and so forth. To cover up the crime of being Jewish, I admitted to minor crimes. I told them that we stole plenty. It was a crime to steal food, but I figured it was such a minor offense that the worst they could give me was a week of camp, a light punishment.

It was forbidden to tear up money. Before getting caught, I had torn up the marks I had. So I told them that. That was a good thing to admit. Marian was supposed to admit that he also tore up the money he stole. We had agreed on these two things.

Then came the moment when I said I was not married to him, that we were pretending to be husband and wife.

"Why?" they asked.

"Oh, we were going out—boys and girls together—that was the reason."

Later on, when I was freed, they separated us completely. I went to a farm and he went to a factory. They even put him in a different village, to make sure. Their morality, their feelings, were terribly shocked.

We were always brought by truck for interrogation. In front by the driver was a special separate compartment for me where I stood closed in behind wires. The others sat on benches. One time, those two German Jewish girls saw me in the truck on the way to the Gestapo.

The one that was not pretty told the policeman, "She is Jewish. She's from Warsaw. I know. I recognize her. She is from Warsaw. She is Jewish!"

How did she know I was Jewish? She did not speak Polish. And she wasn't from Warsaw. The pretty sister started hollering, "What are you saying? You are not helping yourself! Why are you saying that? What for? You want to kill her?"

She was hollering, but the other one kept on talking. The policeman was not paying much attention, but he reported it to the Gestapo anyway. Now they had a lead.

One day, I was sitting, waiting to be interrogated. They brought in a Jewish woman with a yellow star who was also being questioned. An older woman. She had been caught on the train. A German Jewess, she was married to a Gentile man. She had already left her village, but she was still denounced and they caught her.

She still had some sandwiches from the house where she had been hiding and she offered one to me. We each understood who the other was without asking. She spoke into my ear. "You know I have this star that I took off. I have to sew it back on. Do you have a needle and thread?"

I happened to have it and gave it to her. They saw. They had purposely put me with a Jewish woman to see how I would act toward her—if I really would hate her so much and not pretend. They observed and saw that I gave her a needle and thread and that I ate the sandwich she gave me.

When they called me in for questioning, they asked, "Why did you eat food from that Jewish woman? Aren't you disgusted?"

"I was very hungry."

"But from a Jew? To eat? Why did you give her thread?"

"She asked me, but I didn't know what it was for."

"You didn't know?!" they hollered at me.

The next time they tried to trick me into admitting I was Jewish we were cleaning the offices. When we cleaned the floors, we picked up *shtumels,* cigarette butts. We collected them and used them later to make cigarettes with newspapers. Anyhow, there was some Jewish fellow who was working with us. I was sorry for him and gave him a bunch of *shtumels* for a smoke. I made contact without realizing that this Jew was a damn traitor. He was working for the Gestapo.

He came over to me. "What is your name?" he asked. "I am from Wilno. What is your father's name?" He was talking so softly, and with a Jewish accent.

All of a sudden a Polish woman hit me. "Traitor!" she said in Polish. "Not a word to this Jew."

"You Jew!" I said to him. You this and that! I found out
that he sewed suits for the Gestapo men. He was a tailor. He
sewed their clothing, and he translated whenever they needed it. He was a denouncer.

They called me to the Gestapo again. The *Wachtmeister*
who had befriended me came up to my cell. He told me to
be strong. Not to give in. That's all. He could do nothing.
He brought me to the Gestapo office. They made me wait a
long time. The longer you waited, the more scared, the more
panicky, you got. Finally they took me. I had had no break-
fast. I was starving.

There were three men in the Gestapo office. There was
one man who interrogated and beat me. His name was Karl
Krescht. I will never forget that name. There was a translator. And one man who was typing everything we said. The
man at the typewriter looked exactly like my father. He
looked so much like my father that it was upsetting to me. I
saw my father in front of me all the time. I was not supposed
to remember the name Goldberg—but there was my father
right in front of me! How that worked on me!

Krescht showed me a map and asked where I came
from. I made a mistake. I was smart, but I did stupid things,
too. I admitted an understanding of the map. No peasant in
Poland would know that. Many of them did not even know
how to read. They did not know how to read a map for sure.
That was something only someone who was somewhat educated would know. But he showed me the map and asked,
"Where is Warsaw?" Then he asked me about Berlin and
where I came from, and I pointed on the map.

I had already told them I was a peasant, an orphan, but
this time I added a little bit to the story. I said I was an orphan, but I remembered that the nuns who helped me in an
institution said my mother was Ukrainian and my father was
a Pole. That meant if I were to be freed, I would get better
rights. I could go to the movies. I could leave the village and
have more freedom. The Ukrainians were living almost like

free people, like Germans. I had that in mind. I gave them something to think about so they would treat me better.

I was sent to another room. I was alone in this room with another translator, a Polish-Ukrainian. He spoke Polish to me, very sweetly. He was known for torturing prisoners by closing doors on their fingers. He would just close the door. They would use all kinds of systems of torture. Being friendly, nice. Giving cakes, cigarettes. All kinds of ways. Asking you about the others. They would give you the idea that if you denounced someone else, you would be set free.

Once I met a Polish girl in the cell. She said to me, "Remember one thing. Don't ever tell me your name, where you come from, or anything. I don't want to know. I tell you openly. They might beat me tonight. Maybe tomorrow. If they beat me, I will speak. I will say everything about you. Don't ask me anything either, because I don't want you to know a thing about me." And she was not Jewish. I could tell.

She taught me something. She never said, "I know you are Jewish," but she must have known because of the way she warned me. She told me about one Jewish girl from Poland who was caught by the Gestapo and interrogated in a very strong way. After the interrogation she was given a terrific beating. They told her to tell the truth because nothing bad would happen to her. Why not tell the truth? She did and the result was that they hung her from her feet until she died, her own blood killing her.

I knew more or less what to expect. I wondered why that girl was so stupid as to believe the Germans. You could never believe them. They were stupid, but they were always liars and mean. In Poland, in some cases, if you denounced your colleagues, you might have a chance. Never with the Germans. Whatever they said was just a plain lie.

This Polish-Ukrainian translator was actually a torturer, the one who did the beating. Others were mean, but he was the worst. He was famous for his brutality. There was a story of a Russian he had tortured. To get him to talk, this transla-tor had skinned the bottoms of his feet. The Russian walked without shoes and bled on the sidewalk. When this transla-tor spoke softly, it was just before he was ready to torture.

So now, the Polish-Ukrainian translator talked. Under the table they had some buttons. It was all bugged. They knew everything that I said. He said, "I am so tired of this war. I know it's coming to an end. Who do you think will win?"

"What? You're asking me? I don't have a radio. How would I know? The way I see it, the Germans are strong. They are winning. No question about the Germans. They will win."

"Oh, my God," he said. "Don't say that, because I want to be free."

I was sure he was spying.

"How can you say such things?" I replied. "You are working here and you are not for the Germans? You are a traitor. You are a traitor!"

"I am not a traitor. But I will be."

"Oh, my God," I said. "I am not a traitor. I was going to Germany to work and I missed my train."

He made believe he was such a fine man. Then he showed me some cards. When you first looked at the cards, you saw a beautiful Gentile man getting married to a beauti-ful Gentile girl. But when you looked from a different angle, you saw a Jew with a big nose raping the woman. This was to show how bad the Jews were. They were only rapists.

"I don't understand," I said. "What is that?" He was not any friend. I would not have trusted him, even if he had shown me cake instead of that.

"You don't understand? That's a Jew."

Nothing doing. I saw him press something. The rest of the Gestapo came in, walking around and talking to me. They beat me up terribly. Karl Krescht told me clearly, "If you do not talk we will shut the door on your fingers." He beat me on the shoulders and face. I was tortured for such a long time in the most awful way. They would stop only for a second. I wanted water. They put the glass of water down, then took it away. They did not give it to me.

They asked me about the bracelet with camels I had taken with me when I fled our house in Warsaw. The camels made them think it must have some Jewish meaning, that maybe it had something to do with Palestine. I told them I had found it.

The translator was saying, "Tell the truth. Tell the truth. What can happen? You will only go to a camp. What else can happen? Just tell the truth. You can't stand this beating."

The man typing was so upset, he had tears in his eyes. He could not take it either. Maybe they were Nazis, but they could not take it. They were becoming nervous. But I could not trust them too much.

They beat me so terribly that that night, after the beating, I was like pulp. I was different colors. I had a fever. I could barely lie down or even sit I was in such pain. I slept on the floor since there were too many women and not enough bunks. That night on the floor of the cell was terrible. In my delirious state, I almost decided to give myself up. It was the first time that my spirit was broken.

A Polish girl undressed me. She knocked on the door so long that the *Wachtmeister* came. She asked for cold water, which he brought. Ice and cold water. She took her brassiere and her panties and poured water on them and put them on my body.

"I was beaten like this, too," she told me. "Everybody gets this treatment. They want you to admit. Don't confess. Don't admit. Nothing. Tomorrow they won't beat you anymore. I tell you they will not beat you anymore. That's their system. Don't admit. They're trying to break your spirit."

"I don't care anymore," I said. "I don't want to live. I don't want to live."

"No! No!"

I passed an awful night. The next morning was the day of sentencing by the Gestapo. They called one Russian girl. She went out with her fist up, like a communist, and said, "Goodbye. We will meet, and our boys will take care of you." Then, as she passed by a French girl who had denounced me, she said, "I will pass the word that you called her Jewish and you will be finished. When the war is over, you will be finished." I do not know what happened to this Russian girl. She was probably shot.

Then my name was called. The *Wachtmeister* who befriended me told me that I should go to the end of the line.

"For your information," he said, "the Russians are in the town you come from. And they are in Warsaw also. Do you understand what this means? They cannot check you. *Kraft!* Strength! You will come back."

He patted me on the shoulder, and his words prevented me from giving myself away.

When I entered the office of the Gestapo they had sandwiches on the table, delicious sandwiches, cigarettes, matches, water.

"Go ahead and eat," they said. But I could not eat. When I saw that food, I almost cried. That meant I was sentenced to death. Before the electric chair you get everything you want. The food could not go through my throat, nothing. I had a cigarette. Then I got dizzy from the cigarette. Smoking on an empty stomach. It was symbolic: Get whatever you want because you are already finished.

"You were beaten," they said. "We do not want to beat you anymore. You yourself should say whatever you think is right, and then you will be sentenced. Today this is all finished. We do not want to beat you anymore. Do you have something to say?"

"Yes," I said.

"What do you have to say?"

They had taken my two photos—the one of my father

and the one of my nephew, Ronald. The translator looked very strangely at the photo of my father. He seemed quite shocked, and he looked up at me, then again at the photo. This meant that the translator knew my father. He was probably a traitor in the Polish police, or from some other office of the government, a *Volksdeutscher.* I turned to him and said, "You are a Pole. You are not a German."

"I am German," he said. But he was lying. He spoke Polish like someone from Silesia, from Southwest Poland. And he probably lived in Warsaw. I knew his face. It had bothered me from the beginning that I knew his face.

"Look," I said to the typist. "You can write." And to the translator I said. "You translate. My name is not Wrobleska. My name is Irena Olszewska. I am not married. I have a Ukrainian mother and a Polish father. I am Polish. I am Catholic. I am a Jewess. I am a Gypsy. I am English. An American. I was parachuted to poison the rivers of Germany. I am a spy."

They wrote. Then the translator got white. He changed his color when he heard that. But that Krescht was as happy as they come.

"Finally, we got you to talk." And they gave me a paper to sign.

"Before I sign anything," I said. "Read it to me."

Krescht read it. "Now sign," he said.

"No, I won't sign. That I don't sign."

"What do you mean you will not sign?"

"I cannot sign lies. I know that you will beat me. You want me to be a Jewess, a Gypsy. You want me to be a traitor. You want me to be English or American. I am everything, so you can put me in prison or kill me because I cannot take this beating anymore. You want to kill me. I give you all the reasons to kill me.

"But I will tell you the truth. I am Polish from a Ukrainian mother. I wanted to go to Germany to work. I did not mean any harm. I ran away from one place because they beat me up. No other reason. I stole. That man is not my husband. And that's what happened."

They tore up the other paper and wrote out another, which I was supposed to sign. The translator read it, and I checked everything to make sure there was nothing dangerous. But while I was signing, I almost gave myself away. I saw the typist and how he looked so much like my father. Automatically, I almost wrote Goldberg. My name at that time was Olszewska. But I started to make a "G." The translator looked at me with surprised eyes. He understood that something was wrong. But I made the "G" into an "O" and I signed.

Then they said, "We are sorry that you were beaten. We see that you told the truth. We will send you to work. You want to go to work, so we will send you to work. The punishment for running away and stealing was that you got beaten and stayed so long in prison. This is enough punishment. So you will not go to a camp, but back to work."

The next day, who took me to the *Arbeitcentrum* to assign me a place to work but the translator. We were out of the building and on the street when he spoke to me.

"You are a smart girl. You know that I know."

"What do you know?" I asked this translator.

"You know what I know. We both know."

"I don't know what you're talking about. If you are interrogating me again, I'm telling you right now, I don't know what you're talking about. What I told you was the truth."

"All right," he said. "Only one thing I beg of you. Nobody hears us now. The war will soon be over. When the war is over, and the Americans and the English enter, please help me. *Just remember that I did not beat you. Tell them that I am a good German!*"

BLUMENSTADT

I got work on a farm near Erfurt. Erfurt was also called Blumenstadt, which means the town of flowers. Some time ago it probably was a beautiful town full of flowers, but it was near the end of the war when I got there, and the town did not look good at all. America had new bombs, and they were doing saturation bombing. They would finish off one big area, the whole town or half a town, all at once. These were terrible bombs, but for finishing towns they were really marvelous. There were no flowers.

I worked in the farmhouse as a kitchen maid and I milked the cows. Thirteen Italians were there, some couples, some single people. These Italians were all part of a pro-fascist organization, but, as I found out later, at least a few of them were quite against fascism. They had no choice. The only way to keep from going to the front with the army was to go to Germany to work. These people preferred to work than to fight.

Miller, the owner of the farm, was a big drunkard. And he was a big Nazi, definitely pro-Nazi, not a sympathetic family to work for at all. They were very mean. His wife, funny enough, looked exactly like a Jewess. She had a very elongated nose, cheeks sticking out, red, kinky hair, and little bitty eyes. She was so mean to me; she would do everything possible to make my life miserable. When we had to push carts together, I made sure she pushed the most, fooling her into thinking that I was also pushing. Or when we would make sausages, I would steal some of the sausage meat for the Italian girls. When I milked the cows, the Italians would get most of the milk and I would add water to the rest for the farmer's wife.

There were two Italian sisters who were always getting attacked by this farmer, Miller. One of them was younger and prettier than the other. He wanted her, but she did not want anything to do with him. Soon enough he beat up both of them. Then he went to the Gestapo and managed to have them sent to a camp for two weeks. Somehow, because they were strong, they came out of it alive.

There were two organizations that looked after the rights of the farmers and farmworkers of Germany's allies. One was like a station. When they brought you from Poland or some other country, they would assign you work. They decided what was proper for you. If the Italian girls could get to one of these organizations, they would be helped. But no one knew where they were and the Germans would not tell them.

Finally, the girls went to one of these organizations to beg for help, pleading that they were not prisoners of war, they were not against Germany. Furthermore, they said, they were fascists with Mussolini, they were pro-Hitler, pro-Nazi. They begged to get another job because this man was simply a sex maniac. They had nothing against Germany, but they did not want to be with this family.

Do you think it helped? Miller did everything possible to get them both back on his farm so he could beat up the girls in the same way again. These sisters finished the war that way.

Also on the farm was a Polish man from Lublin who looked 100 percent like a Jew, although he was not. He would molest me, bothering me all the time. I would eat in the kitchen, and he would come and put his filthy manured hands in my soup. I could not eat it and would have to throw it out. He was very mean. One day I was working in a barn with a German woman from the village. He came in and out of the blue he said to her, "You know you are working with a Jewess. She is a Jewess." Just like that. I got so panicky I just stopped breathing.

I thought fast. I was lucky and got an idea. I looked at him and said, "He has a Jewish face." I started to laugh very loudly. "Oh, my! Look at him. Look who's talking! I have pity on this man. He is a runaway Jew from the ghetto. Look at the nose, the eyes. Look at the coloring he has. You Germans don't know, but he speaks Polish very badly, like a Jew. He's a Jew, and he dares to talk about me!"

The German woman and the other Germans working there all started to laugh. "What idiots. The Polish people are so funny," they said. "They are so stupid, they quarrel all the time." They did not take it seriously. If they had, you could imagine my position. He repeated the same story to the owner, Miller, but he did not take it seriously either.

The war was coming to an end, but I did not really know it. We were too isolated. One day a young German who spoke some Polish came to the farm. He had cows, and there was one cow—black and white—which was a typical breed of cow in Poland. Germans had mostly brown cows. He had this cow, but it would not give milk. Her udder was all red and swollen, but she would not give milk. By then I knew how to milk, yet I could not get a drop of milk from her.

That man promised me anything, if only I could get the cow to give milk. Otherwise she would die. But she still would not give milk. I got so angry that I hit her and started to curse in Polish. Well, the milk squirted out without me even milking. She gave so much milk that right away she got over her fever. She was a stubborn cow from Poland. She did not like the German people, and she was accustomed to Polish curses. She would give milk only as soon as she heard Polish curses.

The coming of this young man with the cow was a sign to me that the Germans from the Polish side were going deeper back into Germany. It meant they were running away. I remembered a story from my mother and father, of how the Germans ran away from Poland in the First World

War. It was a good sign. All the farms started to fill up with strangers.

One day, a tall skinny fellow I didn't know approached me and said, "Where do you come from?" I was so shocked that he asked me where I came from that I forgot to look at his shirt. Normally, I would have noticed if he wore a "P," which meant he was a Pole, or if he wore "OST," which meant he was probably Ukrainian.

"I come from Rowno," I said in Polish.

"You come from Rowno? *I* come from Rowno!"

I was thinking, "Oh, my God!" I was really from Warsaw, and I spoke with the accent of someone from Warsaw. People from Rowno spoke with a slightly Russian accent because it was close to the Russian border, and they would know Russian or Ukrainian, and I didn't know either one. So I was really scared to death that I had walked into a trap.

"On what street did you live?" he asked.

I didn't know what street I should say—I didn't know Rowno—but then I was thinking there would be some train station there, so I said, "On Kolejowa," which means Train Street.

And he said, "On Kolejowa? *I* lived on that street! What number were you?"

It was just getting worse, but I was thinking number three is my lucky number, so I said, "Number Three Kolejowa."

"Oh, my God," he shouted. "I lived at Number Five!" That would be right across the street. "But I never saw you."

I replied that maybe I was away at the time or was working somewhere else, something like that. I was so scared you have no idea—and then this fellow just disappeared. He could have exposed me, if he was really from there. I don't know why he showed up, and I don't know why he disappeared. He never asked me anything more, and that was lucky because that could have been my downfall, as close as it was to the end of the war. At that time many people were coming and going, showing up and disappearing, the same thing for the Italians, showing up and disappearing. There was confusion because the war was coming to an end.

Meanwhile, we worked in the fields cutting the wheat, but we would leave the root so that it would bloom again. That was sabotage. The Germans were after us all the time. They did not know what to do with us. They never had results with us. But how naive they were. If they had checked how we worked, they would have known immediately that this was sabotage. But they did not use their heads. They only knew how to yell, *"Schnell! Schneller!* Fast! Faster!"* They would just scream at us and then check to see if, God forbid, we got sick and spread disease amongst them!

As the war was coming to an end, the German authorities started to give guns to the little kids who were in *Hitlerjugend,* Hitler Youth. The Millers had a little boy, Wolfgang, eleven years old—about the same age as the *Hitlerjugend* boy on the Albrecht farm where I was first assigned to forced labor. Wolfgang had a gun. If he wanted to kill, he had the right to shoot any prisoner of war or any worker at any time at his pleasure. If he gave an order and the men or women did not do as he wanted, he had the right to take out the gun and kill. This boy had a good time with me. He decided to hold a stick and make me jump over it. I had to jump over it again and again. He would hold the gun and scare me. I jumped like hell, I was so scared! I jumped even though I had a bad leg. A terrible boil, very painful, had festered, and I never got any help from a doctor.

This eleven-year-old boy was studying English. One day he was studying in the kitchen when he made some grammatical errors. He said, "He have."

"No," I said. "You have, I have; he *has."* He jumped up. Here I was supposed to be an ignorant peasant and all of a sudden I was teaching him English. He got furious. He went to his father to say, "She's a traitor. I told you. She speaks English."

"Do you speak English?" the father asked me.

"Oh, no," I said. "I only know a few words." I had made a big mistake, and I had actually endangered myself for no reason.

During alarms, when there was bombing, the farmer would close up the house. They were afraid of thieves. There were prisoners of war, all kinds of people, running away to the fields. At a certain hour—it was like clockwork—we would get the Americans shooting and bombing. No English, no Russians. It was an American zone, and it was the Americans all the time. What a bombing, you have no idea! The planes flew so low we could see the bellies of the planes and even the pilots' faces.

I stayed in the house. I did not want to run out to the fields to go into the bunkers. I would simply stay in the house. I was not scared. I had contacts with French prisoners of war. They would pass by and I would give them cooked potatoes—they were actually for the pigs, but they were good potatoes—and the men would eat extra.

One day, it was getting obvious that the end of the war was coming. It was not easy for me to hear the news on the radio, but when I did I could tell the Nazis knew the war was ending. Miller listened to the radio all the time and knew what was going on. Imagine my surprise when he asked me, "Who will enter? The Americans or the Russians?"

"Why do you ask me? What do I know?"

"But which do you think?" he asked.

"It looks to me like the Americans," I said.

"All the Americans are Jews. All Americans are Jews," he said. "They have a president who is a Jew, Rosenvelt. Still, I prefer to have them than the Russians. The Russians will kill us. That will be terrible. God forbid! Better the Americans. Somehow we will understand each other."

Then he said, "You are a very faithful worker. I tell you what I will do. I'll get you some soap. You need soap." The soap I had was like a stone. I could not wash myself with that junk. I used just water, really, and some soap would have been very good.

"I will give you a cake of soap," he said. "You know, now we get fat from the Jews. Makes terrific soap. It is so soft, it's so good that fingers that are hard become soft from the Jewish fat. This is wonderful soap, really. Thank God we finished the Jews. At least that much we will have accomplished from this war."

I decided there and then and thought to myself, "You sonofabitch. When the right time comes, I will fix you!"

In Erfurt there were Poles from Warsaw, a group captured in the 1944 uprising. The Germans caught the Polish Gentiles but not the Jews. The Jews had all been killed before. Since I was supposed to be half Ukrainian, I had certain rights. I was allowed to go to town. I knew these Poles were making their own vodka, so one day I went to visit them.

They asked me, "Do you want to see somebody very interesting?"

"Who?" I asked.

"We have a Jew with his mother and his child."

The Poles were hiding them. They knew they were Jews, but they did not give them away.

So I went to them after Miller offered me his "wonderful" soap. I said I needed some vodka for my boss who was a good Nazi, an extreme Nazi. This vodka was called *samogonka,* and it was terrible, like poison. They gave me exactly what I wanted.

I was heading back to the farm to take the can of vodka

to him when the Americans started bombing. They always came at about the same time and people knew what to do. It was routine. Every day at three or four o'clock there was an attack. The bombing started and I ran with this vodka. I saw Germans walking slowly. You know how they are so well organized, so calm, that they do not panic, they do not scream. No Jewish-type screaming, just calm Saxon nerves. They walked slowly with their children's carriages, with beautiful cages for their canaries in their hands. They marched out of town peacefully.

I said to myself that I better march faster or I'll get killed. I ran and got to the bridge. All the Russian peasant women captured in Russia, the stupid ones, were sitting on the bridge with their skirts over their heads, thinking they would not be visible, praying. They were not prisoners of war, but prisoners like us. "Get off the bridge! Quick! They will bomb the bridge!" I screamed at them. They did not even answer. They just lay there, waiting and praying. I ran across the bridge like fire.

All of a sudden the whole sky was full of the most beautiful missiles, like kites. The Americans were lighting up flares so they could see exactly every little thing, even though it was three in the afternoon and not dark. I do not know why they did this.

I fell down in the fields when the bombing began. There were all kinds of people who had run away from town. They had had enough and had to run away. The sand covered us from the explosions. Then I ran faster and farther, running so far that I really got myself lost in those fields. There was so much bombing I did not come back to the farm until the next day. I had gotten lost, but I was not running away at this point. I was not in danger like when I was denounced. I had to go back to the farm. I had a bed. No matter how bad it was, it was better than to be hiding in the fields again.

When I came back to the farm, everyone was surprised to see me. They thought I had lost my life. I had this big can of vodka hidden. All throughout the bombing I did not lose that. No matter what, this poison Miller would get!

I gave Miller the can. "I promised you a gift," I said. He thought I was the biggest darling because I had brought him that. He already had drunk his own. Now he drank this can of turpentine vodka with his wife. He finished it and disappeared. We found out later that he was so drunk he took his truck and killed somebody. We did not know exactly what happened, only that before the Americans entered, he was arrested. When the Americans entered, he was in prison for killing somebody. That was how I fixed him for the Jewish soap he told me about.

A few days later, I went back to see Blumenstadt. You have never seen such a thing. I had seen many places bombed. I saw Warsaw—and Warsaw was something to see. But I had never seen so many bombs fall on such a small town. There were houses with four floors. The houses would stand without a roof, only the first floor would remain with nothing in it, destroyed. They were decapitated. Whoever was living on the upper floors had died. They were shoveling the ruins, the Germans, and they would find little children's legs and arms. With so much dirt and ruins, the human beings in this town were turned to powder. Blumenstadt died. That was the end of the town.

"GO TO BUCHENWALD!"

One day, I was left alone in the kitchen cleaning, and stealing as I cleaned. The Germans had left for a few hours, and I looked through the food storage. They had chocolate and all kinds of good things! I was eating and drinking and stealing for my Italian girlfriends. Then I saw their radio. "Oh boy," I said to myself, "here is a big radio." I turned it on.

All of a sudden I heard, "Attention! Attention! We are advising you that whenever there is an alarm for half an hour do NOT go into the fields anymore. Do NOT run to the bunkers again. Stay in the house. If you go to the fields, you will be crushed by tanks." Then I understood that there would be a direct tank attack, no more planes. The announcer continued, "Stay in the basement of your house. Take food for yourself. Stay in the basement when you hear the next alarm. Wait for the alarm. We do not know the exact time, but it may be soon. When you hear a signal for half an hour that means the attack will start directly."

It was the end of the war. When I heard that I started to cry like a baby. "Oh, my God," I said, "you allowed me to survive the war! You really allowed me to survive!" I cried, but I had nobody to tell what I had just heard. I had not seen the French prisoners of war in some time, and I was afraid to tell anyone else because I was not supposed to touch the radio.

Soon after, I was in the kitchen eating my lunch peacefully when all of a sudden I heard the alarm. I looked at my watch, and so did the Germans. It lasted half an hour. "This is the time," I said to myself. "The Americans are coming." I did not know exactly, but I imagined it was the Americans.

Many Germans had come to the village from other areas, trying to escape. Some time earlier that Gestapo man Karl Krescht and all his bunch had shown up. The very man who had tortured me! They would come to the house to eat. Three days before the final alarm they came and stayed in the house. They had prepared a lot of food and drink in the basement. They had said to me, "You must go to the basement. When we say it's time to go to the basement, you come, too." They did not tell me why, but I knew.

After the alarm sounded I thought, "What could stop them from killing me now?" This is toward the end of the war. They can kill me because I know too much. This Krescht had been beating me. He is right there, and he must be afraid of me.

When the alarm sounded, I grabbed certain mementos to prove that my boss was a Nazi. They were trying to throw everything away, insignias, party cards, so that now they could be big friends of America. So I took his party card and I went to the barn. I had prepared myself with a big white sheet. All of a sudden I heard *tutututu,* and I looked through the holes in the barn. American tanks were coming, and they were shooting, but nobody answered. I started to run out with a white flag, running from right to left, screaming and screaming as the tanks came. I thought I would be the first one to open the doors to the town.

One tank got out of formation. It was not shooting. They screamed from afar, "Who are you?"

"Polish! Welcome, brothers!" I was crying and screaming. I was dressed in pants like a man. The pants were in rags and patches. I had wooden shoes. I had some rag on my hair. In front I had no hair altogether. I had one eye smaller than the other. I looked just terrible. The American boys jumped out of the tank. They started to ask questions. There was a Jewish fellow from Brooklyn. I asked if they would stay. No, they were going to Berlin.

"Jump on the tank and go with us."

I said to myself, "First of all, they are men. Let's not go with the men on the tanks! Second thing, Berlin means closer to Poland. Who wants to go to Poland? I want to go to America!" As soon as I had gotten to Germany, I decided that I would never go back to Poland. My sister was in America. But it was not only that. There had been some nice Polish people who had not given me away, and some had helped me. But I had a bad taste in my mouth. I had lost everybody. They were killed because they spoke Yiddish and not Polish. I had lost my whole family. I saw the killing of Jews in the ghetto in the most hideous ways. There was no reason for me to go to Poland.

I tried to remember the address of my sister. She was living in Brooklyn. I had memorized it, but when it came time, I forgot. It killed me that I could not remember. But "Obenzinger," her married name, I did not forget. And I knew "Brooklyn."

So, as I talked to this American Jew from Brooklyn, all of a sudden a woman I had met in the bunkers the times I had gone there instead of into the fields came up to the Americans, screaming. When I had met her there before she had a baby with her. Her child did not talk. It was an abnormal child. Her mother, the grandmother, was always inviting me to her house. I did not know why. "On Sunday, please come to my house," she would ask me. But I heard from other people that she had a big Hitler portrait on the wall. I figured she must be a Nazi, so why should I go to her house? She always brought me sandwiches. During the shooting she would offer me sandwiches, but I would not accept them from her.

Now the woman and her mother started to carry on with the Americans. She was hollering, "I am Jewish! I am Jewish! Not too far from here is Buchenwald! Go to Buchenwald! Save the last ones from death! Go to Buchenwald! Don't waste any time!"

It turned out that they were Jews with false papers. She was married to a German, an officer in the army who was sent to the front. She had this abnormal child, and they had a big Hitler picture on the wall to pretend they were good Nazis. They had all come together from Lodz in Poland. "You did not know," she told me. "I wanted to feed you because you were so hungry. But you were afraid of me." We began to carry on, talking excitedly.

Suddenly, these American boys took me in their hands and started to throw me in the air. Finally I told them, "Please don't throw me so much or you will have not one person but ten. I will fall apart soon." I was too weak and skinny. They did not know what to do for me, but they gave me some stockings. I did not even know how to wear them. I had forgotten about stockings. Then they took out some bottles. They were all drinking and asked me to drink, too. Then they left in their tank.

Now I was in trouble. How could I go back to the Germans? This family could kill me. For a day I stayed there in the fields. But I became hungry. I figured if I went back, the Germans might behave. I also figured they might harm me. I came back just the same, because I had no place to go.

The Americans marched the German Gestapo men, the SS, with their hands up over their heads. I ran after one group. They had one American in front and one in back. In German I screamed, "You German swine! Drop dead!" But it did not really make me feel better. I just had the satisfaction of screaming at them. I no longer had to smile and make believe that I loved them.

By now, the Americans were already in the city, but not yet in the country. In other words, they were very close. My German boss was in prison still. In the house were the grandmother, his wife, and the child, Wolfgang. The grandmother was a very old woman. She had nothing to do with the war. Once, they closed the house during a bombing and I had to take her through the window to save her life. I was sorry for her. She was just a decent old woman. I had no hatred toward her. I would think to myself that maybe somebody was helping my mother, too. I had not gotten any more letters from her since I had asked her to stop writing to me.

Soon the Poles and the Russians tried to beat up their bosses, which was all right with me. My German boss, Miller, was in prison when the Poles and Russians came. The German family ran down into the basement. I spread my hands to save their lives. I wanted to save their lives. I do not know why. I got such a beating from the Polish and Russian people, you have no idea. When they got to the basement they discovered that the family had run away through another door. They had a chance to run away because of me. But actually I ended up also helping this terrible boy, Wolfgang, the *Hitlerjugend*. It was on account of his grandmother that I saved the rest.

That night, I slept in the room with my two Italian girlfriends. I no longer slept in the attic of the German family. I was so accustomed to sleeping in my clothing that I did not even undress. Just as I was, shoes and everything. In the morning, I got up, went outside to stretch, and said, "Thank God. I am alive! The Americans are here. I survived!"

Then I heard something click. It was the gun of a German, a friend of my boss, who had decided to kill me. But my luck was so good that all of a sudden out came Antonio, my Italian friend, Antonio from Padua. I turned around and looked. He twisted the hand of the German, and the gun fell to the ground. Antonio grabbed the gun like a stick and hit the German's head with it. Antonio was very tall. The German was a short man. Antonio knocked a hole in his head, and the German was covered with blood. Then Antonio ran away. He saved my life.

THE CHOCOLATE
SOLDIERS

When I found out the Americans were in town, I went to the American commander. I wanted to find out if they were staying, how the war was going. I was invited to a big lunch with all the American officers. It was the day after the death of President Roosevelt. I did not know anything at that time about Roosevelt, about the Jewish refugee boats he did not let in, about how he would not help the Hungarian Jews by giving trucks to the Germans in exchange for the Jews, and all the rest. To me, at that time, he was a great idealist, a great man.

I came to the lunch. Naturally, I found another Jew from Brooklyn right away. We sat and drank. For me, all this food, and to be sitting with Americans! Yet, with all this, I had never told the Americans that I was Jewish. I was still afraid. But I told this one Jew. I said to him, "Don't tell them, but I am Jewish."

"From where?" he asked.

"From Warsaw."

"Oh, my God, how did you survive?"

"As a Gentile."

He promised not to tell anybody, and he did not tell. I cried quite a bit because of Roosevelt's death, and everyone was rather sad. Amongst these officers there was one with the highest rank, a major or a general, I do not know. We were talking when suddenly he got up and started to scream, "I am in my land! I am German!"

It came out that he was really a German who had come to the United States when he was two or three years old. He was brought up by his parents with very good Germanic feelings and culture. His family was from that area. He was quite drunk, and he was screaming, "Here is where my family is! They are all probably killed! Their houses are burned! All because of the Jews!"

He carried on. Everybody was silent. It was rather unusual for an American officer to speak this way while he was fighting for the freedom of people. They were not just fighting to take the country over, but for a big ideal. It was very unusual. Everybody was upset.

I could not help myself from crying. There was one very tall, very handsome, very blue-eyed officer from Texas. He came over and gave me a sign with his finger. He called me and took me to another room. Then he took me in his arms and kissed me on the cheeks. "Forget it," he said. "He's an idiot. He's a drunk. We don't take him seriously. We're all with you, the people who suffered, and not with him."

That was my first real meeting with Americans. Afterward, I saw Americans going around giving chocolates to the Germans. "Poor Germans, poor German children," they would say. They gave them everything. If they could have given their skin, they would have. The moment the Americans stopped shooting, they started to love the Germans. That was typical of Americans. We called them "the chocolate soldiers." They were funny. Their forgiveness was so fast, it was actually unpleasant. It did not feel right. To be that fast, maybe it was a sign of good Christian people. But to me, it just felt funny. You cannot forget and forgive that fast. I know I didn't. I never will.

FRANCE

I saw that the Americans were staying, but I was already thinking about going to France. I could not remain in Germany. I could always have some enemy like the one who almost shot me that morning. I was quite afraid of the many Ukrainians living there. One day, I was walking toward the city when the Ukrainians started to push me from one side of the road to the other. They did not say I was Jewish, but they were pushing me too much. And I was afraid of bandits. I was really afraid. It was the last moment of the war. There was no bombing, no shooting anymore, but there was still danger and I could be killed by such an accident.

Some of the workers from our farm decided to go to France. We made flags. Everybody made a flag. I had a Polish flag. There was a French flag. There were many flags, many nationalities. There were Italians with us, too. Our German boss had a big truck, so we took this truck. We got gasoline from Americans. We took some bottles and food from storage. We filled up with food. We took clothing, whatever we could. We stole everything from Miller. We had drivers amongst the men. I was the translator for everybody. Nobody spoke English except me. Whenever we needed gasoline, they would stop and I would speak English to the Americans.

But the Americans began to organize themselves. The Poles and Russians and Yugoslavs would come to beat up the Germans, going from farm to farm, house to house, beating Germans. The Germans were beaten right and left. Many were killed. But the Americans gave orders against this because they could not accept that anyone could take justice into their own hands and kill Germans.

157

We ran out of gas at some village. It was getting harder and harder to get gas from the Americans. We went to the mayor of the village and told him, "We want the best food. We want houses, nice bedrooms with clean sheets and everything, and clothing, for sleep and rest. We want to eat dinner and relax."

"No," the mayor said, "we don't have it."

We saw some Americans, a few of them Jewish. "We won't look," they said. "You go beat him up."

That's what we did. We beat up the mayor with sticks. Right away the houses were prepared, everything clean and nice. Food and everything. Whoever would not help, we tore up their curtains and other belongings. We were just paying them back as much as we could.

One night we stayed in a house, and to make sure that nothing happened while we slept, the Americans watched over us. When I opened my eyes, there was a big Negro with big black eyes watching us. I got so scared I almost fainted when I saw him. When I had fallen asleep earlier, there had been some white man standing there. But when I opened my eyes, it was a black man! It was my first contact with black people. I had never seen any in Poland or Germany.

We were getting short on both food and gas. But we finally got to the point near the Rhine where they were sending the French prisoners of war back to France on barges. They were asking whoever was standing in line to get on the barges. "Are you Polish?" they would ask and would not allow you to go if you were. But I was lucky, as usual. I had met some of the French prisoners of war who knew me from the times of potatoes, radio, the news, and suffering together. "She was a very good friend," they said, "and we have to help her." Which they did. When they asked me who I was, I said, *"Je suis française."* They took me for French, and I got on. As soon as we got on the barge, the prisoners of war took their knapsacks and covered me with them as we floated down the Rhine.

Then we got to the train. We sang all the time. All the trains were full of people singing "Oh Madeleine"—all the French songs. "It's a Long Way to Tipperary." I sang the Polish national anthem. It was something like a hundred miles before Paris when the train stopped. They stopped to check the train to see if anybody who was not French had gotten on. The police were starting to check. The first excitement was gone. Now they would go by the law, passports. They got me. They found out I was Polish.

"Why are you on the train?"

"I want to go to France."

"You have to go back. You will wait here for the next train going back to Germany." When he said that, the French prisoners of war began to protest, to scream. They would not go to Paris without me because I was really like a trooper, that I was helping them. They said if you want, take away all the French women who were living with Germans, the ones with shaved heads, those you can take and throw away. So the French Control let me get back on the train.

We arrived in Paris. The station was the Gare du Nord. Here they put the civilians on one side and the soldiers, the prisoners of war, in the center, and there they got me. I was far from my friends. A Parisian policeman asked me, "Who are you?"

I said, very quietly, "I am Polish. But really, exactly, Jewish. From Warsaw."

"Oh!" he exclaimed. "She's Jewish!" It seemed I was the first Jewish woman who came to France. They not only let me in, but when we left the Gare du Nord, they held me up in the air, cheering. I was quite a big hero for them. There were so many people standing outside the gates. They were crying, screaming when they saw me. They were much more excited about me than about their own people. It was so unusual for the French people to see anyone coming back from the camps alive. They would give you seats on the Metro, then. If you were lost on a strange street in Paris, or did not know the language, a policeman would go with you until you got home. If you did not have money, he would pay to get you home. They were not like what you see now. In Paris they are so nasty now. They changed. They forgot all about the suffering, what they and all the others had gone through.

SURVIVORS

In the crowd outside the railroad station there was one Jewish woman from Poland who had been living in Paris for many years, Sonia. I don't remember her last name. She took me to her house. But there were many houses of prostitution in Paris, and the police and the Red Cross were afraid some women would disappear, just get taken without knowing the language or where they were going. So they began to check on Sonia, and I had to go to a Polish camp in the meanwhile.

I went to the camp of the Polish government, which was represented in London during the war. I could have gone to the communist government, but I went to this government because it represented what I believed to be my government. The first thing they did was to bring me to a doctor for a check-up. The doctor said I should drink a lot of wine so I would feel good, because he didn't find anything wrong.

At first I stayed with the common people, and I was so happy to be with Polish people again. But right away, it was "Jewess" here and "Jewess" there, and, "To hell with the Jews." And, "She survived, and how come?" They were ready to kill me.

I grew scared. I saw this was dangerous for me, and I went to the office. They asked me for my name. I gave them my real name. I spoke of my father, because this was the government of my father. Right away, they put me in another part of the camp where there were Polish officers. They gave me such respect, such marvelous treatment. When I slept, they had a special guard for me. They kissed my hand.

"You are the most wonderful person. Your father should have survived!" That was the kind treatment everyone should get in life. It was marvelous treatment, full of love and respect.

They checked Sonia, and everything was all right. I could go back. The officers gave me their addresses. If I needed help, I could come to them anytime. One Polish officer fell for me strongly and wanted to marry me. Naturally, I refused. My goal was to go to America. Nothing else. Not to get involved with anybody.

I went to stay with Sonia. I would often visit the offices of an organization of Polish Jews from Warsaw, where I met Comrade Alexander. It was the Jewish Socialist *Bund,* the *Arbeitring.* It was the funniest thing. All of a sudden, they did not trust me. They thought I was not Jewish. Why? I did not speak Yiddish. My face looked, in their opinion, like a Gentile's. I still wore my cross. They suspected that maybe I was a Gentile, a Ukrainian or a German, who had done some harm to the Jews and I was now looking to hide. I spoke plenty to Alexander and told him where I had lived, what school I had gone to, the teachers I had known. If he did not know these names, he found out from the others. Soon they were sure I was a Jew, and I was at peace.

I was a witness for another girl, who was from the same street in Warsaw as I, but who had gone to another school. She also had papers as a Ukrainian. I said I only knew her from seeing her in Warsaw, but that she was Jewish.

I would stay all day at this *Arbeitring.* I was so accustomed to sleeping on the floor that at the *Arbeitring* I would take a nap under the bench on the floor. They would give us lunch, but we were all very edgy, very nervous.

I met a friend I knew from Warsaw before the war, Dr. Rotbalsam. He had survived the concentration camp because he was a doctor. He told me terrible stories of how people hated him because he always gave them tickets saying that they were healthy, that they could work. They did not realize that if he said they were sick, it meant they were useless to the Nazis and would be killed. He always said they were capable of work, and they were very angry at him. They figured if they got a sick card, they could stay at the camp and rest.

There came a woman to the *Arbeitring*. She was maybe a woman of thirty but she looked like a hundred. All white, wrinkled, with terrible skin. She was sitting with us when suddenly she saw this one man and started to scream, "Traitor! Traitor!" He had probably been a traitor in the camp, and he started to run. In those days, if you were denounced you had a very hard time. The police in France would beat denouncers like hell until they got to the truth of the matter. Many were punished in prison. Many of the concierges in Paris had been big denouncers during the war. They had given away people. Nobody could really hide in Paris. It was not the neighbors who gave you away. It was the concierges who informed for the German police, who worked for the Gestapo.

One day my "husband" Marian Wrobleski showed up. I was amazed. I don't know how he found me, since I was no longer using my false name, or how he managed to get to France. But there he was at Sonia's apartment. However he did it, he knew where to find me, and he came to beg me to take him with me to America. Maybe he had done some crime back in Poland and he didn't want to go back. Maybe he just wanted to go to America. Perhaps he really was in love with me, I don't know. Maybe he thought I was rich and I could help him, but I had nothing. And I did not want to help him if I could. He had said he would tell the Germans I was Jewish, he would have denounced me, and I had had enough of him. I told him to go away, that I never wanted to see him again, ever. Afterward, I felt a little bad. He was strong and I could not have survived without him, especially in the Black Forest. In his own way, he had saved me. But I was done with him forever.

I started to make American friends, like Dorothy Spellman and Malvina Seidner. They were officers and nurses during the war. I met Sydney Eichner, who was a dentist from Detroit. I worked for a summer camp, an orphanage, run by the *Arbeitring* at Le Mans. At the orphanage I could eat better and get fresh air.

The *Arbeitring* looked up families. They had long lists of names on the walls. Somebody would come and find the name of someone who was still alive. I never found a name from my family.

I met a man who worked there, a fellow from Warsaw named Hirszfeld. We got very friendly. He would always say, "Come to my office, I'll give you the news." Hirszfeld himself had come from some camp. He weighed not much more than a bird. When the war was first over, and he realized he had survived, he had started to laugh. He could not stop laughing. They put him in the hospital and put him to sleep. Otherwise he would have died from laughing. Many others were dying from eating. They would throw themselves at the food. I myself would eat from morning to night and in the nighttime, too.

One day when I came to look at the lists I met a woman who had been a girlfriend and schoolmate of my sister. She had come from Auschwitz, I think. She had had the job of pushing people into the gas chambers or into the ovens to be burned. She had put in all her family, her mother, her father, her sisters and brothers. She was altogether crazy because of what she had done. I cannot understand how she could have done it. If it had come to that point, I would have gone with them. But she had really wanted to live— and she did survive. But it was a funny thing, she was more than half crazy. She was always a maniac, aggressive, all the time attacking people. When she saw me, she became hostile. She was furious that I was alive.

I met an American soldier named Leo Zivin. I asked him to write to his family to look up my brother-in-law's name in the telephone book in New York. They found him, not in Brooklyn, but in Manhattan. Nathan Obenzinger, at his business.

Leo Zivin's father called Nathan up and asked, "Do you know somebody by the name of Zosia Goldberg?"

"Certainly," Nathan said. "That's my wife's sister."

"We're calling to tell you she's alive. She's alive and she's in Paris."

"My God! How did you find us?"

"She did not know your address, but she asked my son to ask us to look up your address. That's how we found out."

He gave Nathan my address. Then Nathan told my sister. "Roma," he said, "I advise you to sit down. You might fall over when you hear what I have to tell you. I have good news. But sit down."

"What's the matter with you?" She sat down.

"Zosia is alive."

She started to scream good and proper.

Then Roma went to Simon Cohen. His wife was a first cousin of my brother-in-law. They were invited to dinner. Simon Cohen said, "You know, I have a paper, the *Forward,* and they say something about how Zosia Goldberg survived. Who is this Zosia Goldberg?"

"That's my sister," Roma said.

"I am going to Paris," he said. "I'll see what I can do to bring her over to the United States."

Then one day, before Simon arrived, this friend of mine, Hirszfeld, made a signal for me to keep quiet. "Don't tell anybody. We got news of a Stefania Goldberg. Her maiden name was Gurfinkiel. She's from Krakow, but she used to be from Warsaw, she says. She is looking for her daughter. Stefania Goldberg is announcing that she is alive."

"My mother! How can you be sure? Stefania Goldberg, Gurfinkiel, that must be my mother! She was from Warsaw, and during the war she was in Krakow!"

"That's what I thought. But now, when you go out,

don't show your feelings because they will go crazy, all these people looking for their families. So far nobody has found anybody, and you are the lucky one. So you'd better keep quiet or they will be terribly jealous."

I sent my mother a letter giving my address in Paris. I told her I was already in touch with Roma in the United States, and that I was going there. I told her to wait, that we were arranging for someone to come get her. Simon Cohen was already in Paris, and he had paid someone in the American embassy $2,000 to bring her. To make sure she got the letter, I wrote on top of the envelope, "Stefania Goldberg, alias Dimka," the last name she had used during the war.

My mother was staying at the house in Krakow where she had worked for the Austrian and Czech family. The family had run away to Germany and they had wanted to take her with them. She stayed in Krakow, naturally. Not only had she survived, she had seen the Germans leave and the Russians come in. When the postman came with my letter, he said to my mother, "Is your name Stefania Goldberg?"

"No," she replied. She was still too afraid to admit it. On the envelope I had written that the postman who delivered this mail would get some money if he made sure it was delivered to her and then wrote us a letter of confirmation. So the postman was very anxious to deliver that letter. But, still, my mother would not admit her name. He was smart, this postman. He took a good look at her. He saw the black eyes and hair and figured she was Jewish. "Here is the letter. Do whatever you want with it." And he gave it to her. He wrote me confirming delivery, and I sent him the money.

With the escort arranged by Simon Cohen, my mother left Krakow and went through Czechoslovakia, through the United Nations' refugee camps, until she got to France.

One day I got a letter from my mother, which she had sent in reply to mine. I was in Sonia's house when Alexander gave me the letter. I screamed so loud that all the neighbors ran to our apartment to find out if somebody had died. I was laughing and screaming and crying.

Meanwhile, Simon Cohen was taking us out—Dorothy, Malvina, Sonia, everybody—to dinner, drinking, dancing, getting crazy. Then came the Fourteenth of July, Bastille Day. On this day of liberation there were big parades. I went with Dorothy and Malvina to the Champs Elysées, walking there, and we sat down with some French people drinking wine, very happy. But when night came, some American officers, MPs, came by. "Our American girls with these French men? This is too dangerous," they thought. "We will take you girls to the compound," they said. And they took us away by force. The French men were completely inoffensive. They were just happy, singing, nothing else. But that was how our day of liberation was cut short.

I had to get my papers in order before I could leave. By that time the communist government of Poland had prevailed, and the other government's offices had closed. In order to go to America, I had to have what they called a *visa de sortie* from France. For this, I had to have permission from the Polish embassy.

But first they had to make me a passport. When I came to the embassy and they asked my name, they were already calling me "comrade." I was calling myself *"panienka,"* which means Miss. When they called me comrade, I said, "Please don't talk to me like this. I am nobody's comrade."

I noticed in the communist embassy that when somebody came who had been a traitor during the war, sure enough, the embassy's doors closed shut behind them. The traitors never left the embassy. The Polish authorities fixed them. What they did, I do not know. In all respects, they left me alone, and they made me a passport.

I already had permission from the French authorities to leave. But when it came to getting the exit visa, the Polish government said no.

I had gone back to the Polish embassy with Simon

Cohen. He got so furious with these lower dignitaries who denied my visa that he started to scream. Someone said to Simon in English, "You can do that in America but not here. You are in the Polish embassy and don't forget it." They were ready to arrest him. But after a long struggle with them, I finally got to speak to the ambassador.

"My dear girl," the ambassador said to me. "What is your education? Did you finish school in Poland?" He asked me many more questions.

"Look," he said. "We need people with high-school diplomas, with some kind of formal education. Right now, after the Nazis, we don't even have people who know how to write. It will take us a very long time to turn out people with education. Never mind those with university degrees, they don't exist. The Germans cleaned them out. Priests, engineers, doctors, they all went. Finished. Very few are left. We need everyone who has some kind of education. At least you could teach primary school classes. We need people. We cannot permit Polish people to go to America just like that."

"I don't think you realize I am Jewish," I responded. "I have nobody in Poland. They have all been killed. The ghetto does not exist, the people are gone. My friends don't exist. Nobody. I don't want to go back to Poland. I have one sister in America, at least someone from my family. In Poland I have nobody. I think I have a right after this war to go where I want to go."

"You are right," he said. "In that case, I give you permission."

Simon left for London. He sent me a telegram that I should not worry. About two weeks later, I got my visa. I was called to the American embassy. I was going on a little boat, a schooner called the *William Jerman*. Then I went to Bordeaux to board the ship.

The schooner was waiting, taking several days to load. Alexander said, "When your mother comes, I'll bring her to the boat so you will have a chance to see her." I knew that she was supposed to come from the train at a certain hour. I looked on all sides, wondering where my mother was. If Alexander had not been standing with her, I would never have recognized her at all, she was such a changed woman. She had become a very old woman, her face so wrinkled, so terrible. She looked so horrible. When she came over to me, she had not recognized me either. That was our meeting. She would come to America later. She spent one day with me. The next day I sailed without her.

During that day my mother told me her story, how she had spent the rest of the war in Krakow, the maid of a Nazi family, taking care of their child. The father worked as an engineer on the trains.

They never knew she was Jewish, although they had come close to finding out. She was always teaching Catholics how to follow their religion without knowing anything herself. She liked that—giving advice. One day, around Christmas time, she said to the Czech wife that in Poland they never put wreaths up in the windows. This woman thought it was strange that a Pole would not hang a wreath at Christmas. Plus, my mother did not speak German. She spoke simple Yiddish to the Czech woman, and at first the woman figured this was broken German, but then she started to suspect something.

My mother was still sending me letters at that time, and the woman decided to check on the person my mother was sending letters to. She got news from the Gestapo in Germany that I was under suspicion of being a Jew.

So the family started to check her. She would have been in big trouble. If the Gestapo had beaten her as good as I had been beaten, she would have sung. She would have told them everything and more. But she was really lucky.

Remember, after we left the ghetto one of the first apartments we went to in the Aryan section was one where they made false papers. We had given a diamond ring to the forger in exchange for papers. But he had cheated us. The papers were very badly made, and we had to throw them away because the Germans would know right away they were false.

My mother had wanted a *Ken Karte,* the registration card everyone had to carry that had a three-quarter view photo showing the left ear and the nose to indicate how Semitic you were. One day in Warsaw, after we had separated, she had gone to some bureau without any papers. She saw somebody who spoke Polish. "I want to tell you something," she told him. "I am from the legions of fighters for the independence of Poland ..." Whatever my father had done, she said that she did. She said she was from another town and had lost her birth certificate. She offered money. She had a lot of nerve. I would not have done that—gone to the police and asked them, "I want to make an ID!"

"What name should I write?" he had asked.

"Any name will do. You are a Pole."

Actually, he was probably a *Volksdeutscher.* But the way she came, with such assurance, he did not even think twice that she was not a Gentile. He was sure. He believed her. Not only that, but he figured he would get good money, which he did. She had sold some of the gold I had left with her.

"It'll take some time," he said. He was the one who found her the name of Dimka. He found somebody who was dead and he got the birth certificate, then he made really legitimate papers.

So, by the time the Czech woman started to investigate her, she really had a *Ken Karte.* It would have been very hard to check that. It was war, after all, and the Polish government had burned up a lot of papers. It would have taken a long time to discover that this person, this Dimka, was not alive.

The woman did all this checking when her husband was away. She harassed my mother, mistreating her, not giving her food, keeping her in a cold room. She made her sleep on the balcony, even in winter. She would take advantage of her whenever her husband left for Germany. When he came back, he stopped her. He asked my mother why she had such a sad face when she worked. "She is killing me. She is doing everything possible so that I should suffer. She doesn't even give me food."

He scolded his wife and told her to stop this nonsense, and she stopped. Then they lost track of me in Germany, so they couldn't check on me anymore. I already had another name and was in a different town. I had known that because of me, she'd be in danger too, so I had decided not to write anymore. I was already compromised, and I did not want her to get into trouble because of me. I already figured that I would be killed. I had lost confidence. But she figured she was fine. She had good papers. How could she lose her life because of me? It was like when that man caught us in Warsaw and I gave her signs to go away and she wouldn't. She did not believe me. That was my mother.

In any case, the woman she worked for lost her life in the last moments of the war. She died a very sick woman. Then one day the Russians came to Krakow. My mother was in the apartment when in came a big Russian. She was scared of him. But all of a sudden he said to her, "Do you speak Yiddish?" He was a high officer! She could not get over that he was a Jewish officer. She was overjoyed. Until then, she did not know what would happen. In many cases, the Jews were afraid to register their names, and it was very hard for Jews to find each other. They were afraid of Ukrainians, of Poles, of anybody, afraid they would be killed. So they would not register. But she was lucky that she found a Jewish officer, because then she registered with the authorities. That's why I found her.

THE WILLIAM
JERMAN

I went to the United States, to Philadelphia, in the little boat called the *William Jerman*. We made part of the voyage tipped to one side. The boat nearly sank. The ship was not safe, and there were still mines in the water. It was very dangerous.

But there were other things that troubled me. The captain was an Englishman, and the first officer was a Polish Gentile. There were thirteen passengers. Amongst them was a woman from the French embassy going to the United States. She and I were sitting down at the same table to eat, and she said simply, "I am not going to sit with a Jewess." This was the end result of Hitler's influence.

The captain, when he heard that, came over to my table. "May I have the honor to invite you to my table," he said. He made me honored to be there. I had eyes full of tears. It was already after the war and I did not want to hear that hateful talk anymore. The Polish first officer spent all his time with me. To make me happy, he would dance with me. Whenever he was off duty, he danced with me.

There was also an American Catholic priest who became a friend of mine. He was always telling the officers to go over and dance with me. He was like a matchmaker, this priest. He was born in America, but he was of Polish descent. He spoke English, Polish, German, French, Greek, Hebrew, Italian—I don't know how many more languages. A highly educated man, a linguist, who spoke beautifully in any language. Right before the war, without realizing that there would be a war, he had gone to see the country of his parents and grandparents. While he was in Poland he had gotten caught in the war. The Germans sent him to Dachau.

They sent many priests to Dachau, and he survived only because he was an American. I told him the stories of what I had gone through.

"My dear child," he said. "Don't feel sorry for yourself all the time. Other people went through horrible things, too. You have to keep on living." He gave me spirit.

He told me a story. The Nazis put priests in barrels of cold, icy water up to the nose in the frost of winter. They were submerged in the water, including their mouths, so they could not talk to each other. Then they would put them in lines, giving them whips, so that one priest had to whip the priest in front of him. Then they would be sent back to the water. With tortures like this, virtually all of the priests died over there. Before a Catholic dies he makes his last confession to a priest. He became the Father Confessor for all of them. He only survived because he was American.

He told me once, for no reason, that he didn't have any money. I said to the other passengers that we needed to take up a collection for this priest. The French gave some. Somebody else gave some. I had some gold coins and I gave them, too. The rest did not want to give to him because they were Protestants. The cutest thing I ever saw!

When it comes to money, people are nasty. Everything up to money is fine, but when it comes to money, it's finished. Whenever this priest prayed and gave sermons, they would not come. Only once did they come, when the boat was on its side in a storm. They got so scared, they figured they better be nice to him because he had connections with God.

With the boat always close to sinking—with all that had happened to me—I was simply lucky to get to Philadelphia. Simon Cohen was waiting for me, along with my brother-in-law Nathan and my cousin Benny. As I walked off the boat, Simon Cohen said, "Kiss the dirty earth before you step down!"

So I bent down and kissed the dirty earth. Properly.

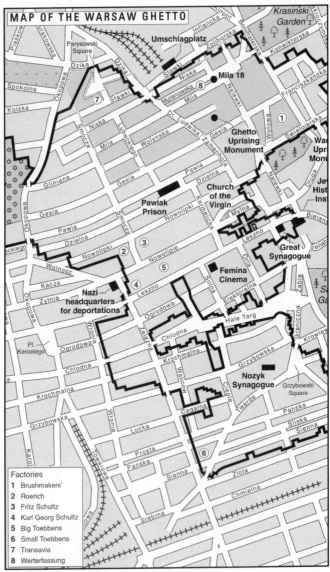

MAP OF THE WARSAW GHETTO

Factories
1 Brushmakers'
2 Roerich
3 Fritz Schultz
4 Karl Georg Schultz
5 Big Toebbens
6 Small Toebbens
7 Transavia
8 Werterfassung

Map published by permission of Martin Gilbert, author of *Atlas of the Holocaust,* Third edition (Routledge, London and New York, 2002).

PHOTO
SECTION

Mother, Zosia, Roma, Father—Warsaw, c. 1932

Zosia at French Cedib School for Cosmetology—Warsaw, 1938

Zosia, second from right, in *Gymnasium* class—Warsaw, 1937

Zosia with sister Roma and her husband Nat—Vistula River, 1938

Back: Zosia and Roma. *Front:* Nathan Obenzinger, Roma's husband, alongside Zosia's parents. Photo taken during Nathan and Roma's visit from America after their wedding—Warsaw, 1938

Zosia on Warsaw street before invasion—1939

Zosia on Warsaw street before invasion—1939

Zosia and mother at the grave of her father—Warsaw, 1940

Stefania and Zosia Goldberg's German ID photos—1945

Zosia, known at the time as
Irene Wrobleska, posing for
German ID—1945

Zosia with Simon Cohen,
who came to Paris to bring her to America, and Sonia—Paris, 1945
*Note: Zosia wears a German dress taken from the wife
of the farmer where she did forced labor*

Sonia and Zosia with American soldiers—Paris, 1945

Meeting of socialists and communists.
From left, seated at table: Pola Maslo, resistance hero; Leo Zivin, Zosia,
unknown man, and Comrade Alexander—Le Mans, 1945

Two American nurses who became Zosia's friends,
Dorothy Spellman and Malvina Seidner Leiner—Paris, 1945

Dorothy, Sonia, Dr. Rotbalsam, Zosia, and Hirszfeld—Paris, 1945

Zosia's mother, unknown woman, and Sonia, seeing Zosia off
before she sailed to America—Bordeaux, 1945

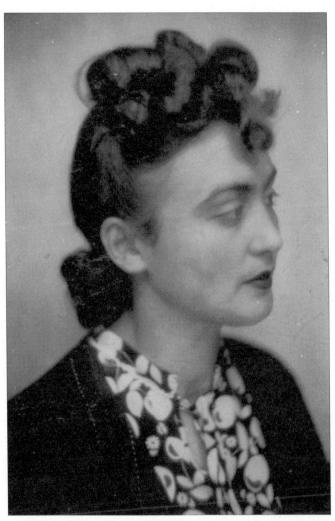

Paris, 1945

ABOUT THE AUTHORS

After surviving World War II, ZOSIA GOLDBERG came to the United States, married, then moved to Caracas, Venezuela, to operate a garment business. She returned to America after her husband's death and currently resides in Florida. She has one son.

HILTON OBENZINGER is a poet, novelist, and critic, and a recipient of the American Book Award. His book *Cannibal Eliot and the Lost Histories of San Francisco* was published by Mercury House in 1993. He teaches American literature and honors writing at Stanford University.

PAUL AUSTER's work has been translated into thirty languages. Following *The Book of Illusions,* which was a national bestseller, his newest novel, *Oracle Night,* was published in December 2003. Celebrated for works such as *The New York Trilogy* and *Timbuktu,* he is also the author of three screenplays (including *Smoke*), and the editor of the NPR National Story Project anthology, *I Thought My Father Was God.* He lives in Brooklyn, New York.